CONFESSIONS OF AN ORGANIZED HOMEMAKER

The secrets of uncluttering your home and taking control of your life.

DENIECE SCHOFIELD

CONFESSIONS OF AN ORGANIZED HOMEMAKER

The secrets of uncluttering your home and taking control of your life.

DENIECE SCHOFIELD

BETTERWAY BOOKS
Cincinnati, Ohio

Other fine Betterway Books are available from your local bookstore or direct from the publisher.

03 02 01 00   12 11 10 9

Library of Congress Cataloging-in-Publication Data

Schofield, Deniece
    Confessions of an organized homemaker : the real secret of
uncluttering your home and taking control of your life / Deniece
Schofield.—1st ed.
        p.   cm.
    Rev. ed. of: Confessions of an organized housewife. 1st rev. ed. 1982.
    ISBN 1-55870-361-6 (pbk.)
    1. Home economics. 2. Housewives—Time management. 3.
Homemakers—Time management. I. Schofield, Deniece. Confessions of
an organized housewife. II. Title.
TX147.S36   1994
640—dc20   93-41641
                                                        CIP

Edited by Donna Collingwood
Cover illustration by Ursula Roma

PART FIVE

Conclusion......................................204

INTRODUCTION

All my literate life I wondered whether I would get a chance before I died to use the word *hugger-mugger*. I wonder no more. *The state of our house years ago made it obligatory.*

You needed a camel, a canoe, a priest and a tourniquet just to get through it. We had three kids under age 4, a dog with a penchant for chasing motorcycles, and a washing machine that headed south whenever it was running.

I wasn't lazy. On the contrary. I was always busy straightening a mine field of Barbie dolls, multicolored skateboards, tennis balls, squirt guns and Big Wheel bikes. I could never understand (since the house was decorated in early memorandum) why I forgot appointments and continually ran out of things like bread, paper towels, notebook paper and light bulbs. More than once I left a soccer team starving for oranges because I forgot it was my turn to bring refreshments to the game.

I was constantly moving from one mess to another, rarely finishing anything before the next crisis was tackled. It seemed like I was just following my kids around trying to keep up with their piles of discarded toys, clothes and food crumbs. I was like a hubcap spinning for the gutter.

I knew the principles of organizing. I could even put them to use when I was at work. But at home, life was a series of unwashed dishes, unanswered letters, and unsightly piles of dirty clothes.

I decided to attack the problems head-on. I tried and re-tried various techniques, refined and adapted numerous strategies, and found many new solutions to old home management problems. Soon I was able to handle my housework while enjoying the freedom I needed and wanted for other activities.

If you're like me, you not only need motivation to get going; you need to know exactly what to do. This book will address both needs. It's packed with ideas that will help you take control of your own house.

WHAT DO *YOU* LIKE TO DO?
Maybe you'd rather spend time in the backyard painting the sunset, digging in the garden, or playing tetherball with the kids. Me too. That's exactly why I decided to get organized in the

first place. Like it or not, we all must do at least a modicum of housework. Organizing is the means whereby we can streamline those necessary chores, so we can get on with life's more pleasurable experiences. Discretionary chores are much more satisfying and enjoyable than those reminders on the mind's periphery regarding the chaos, disarray and disharmony caused by undone chores.

I enjoy an organized lifestyle, because it helps me get what I want. Good home management skills provide me with a cheerful background for living. A well-managed home eliminates much tension and irritability. There are fewer interruptions. Because things are orderly, minimal time is spent housecleaning. I have a lot of free time while I still enjoy the benefits of a tidy, comfortable home. From this viewpoint, housework doesn't seem so bad, does it?

So, you spend most of your life studying rapid eye movement or maybe you specialize in Asian drug smugglers. Domesticity sort of pales by comparison. However, if you feel that you should do a better job at home but can't because you just don't like to do the work, try this. For a short time concentrate on doing it better. When you do something really well, you generally enjoy doing it. What's your passion: What do you love to do? I love to do handwork, and I can do it really well. I don't enjoy sewing. I'm only a fair sewer. My son doesn't like to read. He doesn't read very well. My husband loves to shovel snow. At the first sign of a single snowflake he's out there.

Just think about this for a minute. What do you like to do? Chances are ten to one that you do those things pretty well, don't you?

I have put this to the test many times. For example, once I was put in charge of a school carnival. The date of the event was several months away, and already I was dreading the time and energy it was going to take to put this carnival together. The overwhelming nature of the project caused me to procrastinate it. All the while my dread and loathing for the task grew. Then I decided to follow my own advice and try a different approach. I concentrated not just on getting the job done, but on doing it *better*. At first I had to force myself to get busy. I researched ideas, interviewed people who had preceded me, and started assembling a file of ideas. Gradually, I secured a staff of volunteers. Before long a funny thing happened. The roiling stomach and the stress and tension I had experienced gave way to excitement and a feeling of challenge. My approach worked. I did the job better, and I grew to like it.

Don't sit around waiting for your mood to change. Act differently first, then your mood will follow along. You can act yourself into feeling differently.

HOUSEWORK AS A TOOL

What you need to do is to put housework in its proper perspective. View it as a tool to help you get what you want. Don't visualize youself as a dismal failure. Instead, visualize yourself lying down every night with a peaceful feeling, knowing your work has been done well. You awaken to a house that is in order. The washing has already been sorted and pretreated. The dishwasher (or sink) is empty, and you know what you're going to fix for dinner that night. While you are busy with your morning duties, you are rarely interrupted, because your family can easily find the things they need.

You'll even be more effective and cooperative at work when you walk out of a smooth-running home in the morning. Your mind is free to focus on business projects when it's not hampered by whisperings of "don't forget" or "I should have."

Sure, things will spill and cars won't start. There will still be life's little emergencies and unexpected interruptions. (You may even have some of life's big emergencies!) But even with setbacks, you'll be in better shape than the depressed soul who awakens realizing there is no milk for breakfast; you have no clean clothes for work; and Michael can't find his shoes for school!

I know this from experience, because I have been both of these home managers. I have felt the thrill of victory and the agony of defeat, and I'll take the thrill any day.

You can become a happier, more cheerful you. How? Keep the vision of the "all together" you in your mind. You have to see yourself succeeding before you ever will. If your mind has a positive goal, your body will follow along.

However, as long as you have a negative goal, you will continue to drift along in a negative manner. The old axiom, "accentuate the positive, eliminate the negative," really pays off in the long run.

Make up your mind *right now* that it really is possible to become the person in your dreams. Remember, success starts the very minute you do. Put to use some new ideas and you will see your drudgery turn into pleasure. Why? Because after getting things organized you will have much more time for you!

WHAT'S YOUR EXCUSE?

More than likely, you feel there is a very good reason that you're not as organized as you'd like to be. Because I've had the opportunity to teach and talk to so many people, I think I've heard every excuse in the world! Check to see if yours is included in this list:

- "I've got too many kids."
- "I have all these preschoolers."
- "I have teenagers."
- "The kids un-organize faster than I can organize."
- "My spouse is a slob."
- "I don't have a spouse."
- "I have a job outside my home."
- "I don't have enough time."
- "There's not enough storage space in my house."
- "I'm always tired. I don't seem to have any energy." (One droopy-eyed woman complained to me, "I'm not a day person, and I'm not a night person. My husband wants to know what *am* I a person?")

While these may be valid reasons for slowing down, they are not valid reasons to stop. The only thing that can stop you is *you!* There's a *u* in every ex*cu*se. Start substituting action for explanation. Somewhere there's a person with circumstances similar to yours who is organized and efficient. If someone else can do it, so can you.

Let me introduce you to Jennifer. You might say I sort of worshipped her from afar. She was the quintessential homemaker: four well-groomed, polite, intelligent children; tidy house and yard; efficient volunteer at school and church. She didn't have all the trials I had, so I thought. Then I got to know her better. First, she suffered from pernicious anemia, so she was constantly feeling fatigued and battling for her health. She worked full time as a librarian. Her small home continually put her organizing skills to the test. Then, of course, she had the usual time demands of wife and mother, career woman and volunteer.

Here's my point. No matter how hard you think you have it, there is someone out there worse off than you are who's managing to overcome trials. Excuses are retarding. They keep you from reaching the full potential of your dreams.

So, dump your excuses. You have so much to gain by reaching for your new vision.

As you begin to place the things around you in order, you may very well feel like all your time is being absorbed. Don't give up. Work at getting organized like a hobby. Set aside a certain amount of time each day (or whatever your time budget will allow). While it may indeed take a fair amount of time to establish order, once it is achieved, you will save more time than you have ever spent.

There are so many things I love to do that I'm constantly striving to become more organized, so I'll have more time to do them. I have my schedule set up so that I have three days a week that require some housecleaning. The other four days are my days off when we simply maintain what's been done. The more efficient I am, the more time I have to pursue my particular interests.

Although I consider myself fairly organized, I have days when I set about my work haphazardly, hence my efforts are wasteful. By evening on such days I'm usually deciding that the bathroom can wait until tomorrow and I can always wash later. On the other hand, if I move systematically and consistently through the house, I can be completely done with everything hours sooner and feel lifted up instead of burdened and defeated.

I point this out for two reasons: First, I know from my own experience that organizing does pay rich rewards in extra time and a fantastic sense of well-being. Second, I also know that even an organized person has days that aren't efficient and well managed. So, don't be too hard on yourself when you mess up.

If you are an extreme case (we all are, once in a while), try just one new idea at a time. Move to the next idea only when you feel you have mastered the first. Whatever you do, don't throw your dishwater hands in the air and claim disgust, defeat and insanity! (No matter how efficient I am, though, there are days when I feel like doing just that!)

Often we say, "I have to get out of this house!" Or, "I have to get away!" When I have things running smoothly, our home is the happiest, most peaceful place I know.

The best moments in life are those moments when you feel in control. When things at home are running smoothly and you're released from those pangs resulting from undone or haphazardly accomplished responsibilities, your self-confidence doubles and affects every facet of your life. You will see your effectiveness increased, your energy boosted, and your physical and mental capacities increased. When you're on top of things, your attitude says, "I'm doing a good job. I can handle anything that comes my way today." It's exhilarating. At first you will feel the confidence boost from inside yourself. Soon, other people will notice the "new you" and start to comment on it. That's when you really become motivated.

Being organized will give you more free time, contribute to a cheerful nature, and add to the peace and security of your home. If you want these conditions badly enough, it is worth all the strength you can muster to work at it. Remember that the extreme of being organized—being over-organized—will make you and your family a miserable conglomeration of nervous wrecks. Efficiency is good only when it works *for* you, not *against* you. So, find a level of efficiency that works well for you and *use* it.

Today more than ever before, we have a wealth of opportunities and adventures at our fingertips. Organized living will give you all the time you need to make the most out of every chance.

PART ONE

ORGANIZATION AS A WAY OF LIFE

CHAPTER ONE

A House That's Always Clean

G one are the days when the quintessential "woman of the house" flowed from room to room, cleaning every corner while dressed in a tidy frock complete with jewelry, makeup and high heels. If you're like me, you probably never felt like you quite measured up.

Today, however, a much more realistic standard is depicted in the media. Turn on any show, and you'll see notes stuck to the fronts of refrigerators, kitchens messed with meal preparations, bulletin boards at full capacity, and an occasional unmade bed. Somehow it all seems to make real life more acceptable.

As I speak to people around the country, I see three distinct types: First, there are those who battle unceasingly to have a house that's always clean. Second, there are those who have formed their family members into a cooperative legion where everyone pitches in and takes responsibility for specific areas. Last, there are those who don't care what gets done. They just don't think home management is too important.

If you see yourself in the first category you may frequently overhear, "Oh, their house is always clean." Then you cringe a little inside wishing that it were your house they were talking about.

Well, just to set the record straight, there is no such thing as a house that's *always* clean. Even a house with no occupants gets dirty. Even a museum needs to be cleaned. Yet there is something in your psyche that tells you, "a house that is always clean is my goal." That one little idea causes so much discouragement. You need to realize that no matter who "they" are, or how they clean, their houses are sometimes a mess, too.

It's pointless to compare yourself to other people. I am 5 feet

7 inches tall. Because my sister is 6 feet tall, does that mean I am short? Certainly not. It simply means that we are different.

When we had five children at home eating in the kitchen every day, I usually wiped up the floor on a daily basis. Someone without children could wipe up the floor once a week or maybe once a month. Circumstances and lifestyles vary too much for accurate comparisons. The only effective measuring stick is to compare where you are today with where you were six months ago. Don't ever compare yourself to anyone else.

We tend to see ourselves at our worst, while we see others at their best. When you walk into a neighbor's house, you see a shining entryway and formal living room. Automatically you assume their entire house is in the same condition. Then your mind flashes back to the state of your own house. Maybe your entry and living room are showplace perfect, too, but all you can visualize is the sorted laundry lying in front of the washer. You remember the fingerprints on the French doors, and immediately you feel inferior to your friend. You jump to the conclusion that he or she is a better manager than you are. How someone else's home looks simply does not matter. What does matter is that you have a happy, comfortable home and time to do the things you love to do — not just the things you *have* to do.

Maybe you have a crew of willing workers who know their jobs and perform them well. Maybe you don't care a whole lot. Wherever you're coming from, a certain semblance of order and hygiene is required. Otherwise the neighbors may complain, and the press may show up looking for a story on how you live the way you do. The only way to keep things going and to keep our names out of the paper is through the labor of housework.

Outcries against housework are becoming more and more common: "It is boring. It is unfulfilling. It is monotonous. It is never done. I hate to do over today what I didn't even want to do yesterday."

The reason we feel this way is that we take on home management with little or no training. We have to learn through experience, through trial and error. It's not mentally stimulating. No wonder housework becomes a drudge!

Using the basic organizing principles discussed in the next chapter, you can learn to simplify housework, so it takes less time and energy and becomes less of a grind. You will then be free to do more important things. Also, as you start to look for short-cuts and ways to apply the basic organizing principles, *those* things occupy your mind and make those mundane household chores more mentally challenging. No longer is it just "the same old thing." By using these principles you can schedule your work conveniently. Your improved attitude may very well attract other family members so they will begin to consider home management a science, not just "woman's work."

HOUSEWORK DOESN'T HAVE TO BE UNREWARDING

One of the reasons housework seems unfulfilling is that our methods are often inefficient and wasteful. Plan your work by looking for better ways to accomplish it. That alone will raise housekeeping from the class of the mundane and put it into the scientific class, and your work will become more challenging.

Housework can also be unrewarding if it seems endless, as it often will to the perfectionist. If you're a perfectionist, you need to know when to stop. Remember, there are more important things in life than housework.

Being a perfectionist is extremely inefficient. Let me show you three real-life examples. Perhaps seeing these will help you see the folly of your ways.

I am personally acquainted with three perfectionists. One of them irons shoelaces. The second one scrubs the garage floor with bleach once a week. The third misguided soul changes the sheets on her son's bed once a week. Now, if that boy were still living at home, changing his sheets once a week would seem reasonable. But, he's been married and gone for three years now! Here's just one more—sort of a bonus fourth—I can't resist sharing with you. I know a woman who turns her throw rugs upside down (so the rubber side is facing up). She only turns the right side up when the "good company" comes.

WHAT PRICE PERFECTION?

What is your perfectionism costing you? Time, mostly, but you are paying in other ways as well. You can stifle creativity by providing too sterile an environment. One man I know has a perfection problem. On several occasions his children have set up a game and gone back to the toy room to get a missing piece. While they were gone, he'd quickly put the game away.

You can make people feel uncomfortable and unwelcome when they're allowed to walk or sit only on plastic. Your desire for perfection can also be costly to your nervous system. You've probably heard about the woman who goes to bed with string mops attached to both feet. That way, if she has to get up during the night, she can be accomplishing something!

If you see yourself in these examples, learn to relax and try to do one job imperfectly every day. You will save hours just by changing your standards. Life is too short to worry about yellow, waxy buildup.

I heard a quote once that I often repeat to our kids: "Fun is an *attitude*, not an activity." No matter what set of circumstances surrounds you, a simple attitude adjustment might be all you need to get yourself going.

CHAPTER TWO

The Basic Organizing Principles

The ultimate purpose of organizing your home and your life is to give you time for more important things. Whether you want to be climbing mountains in Nepal or crocheting afghans, work simplification techniques will give you a clearer path to pursuing your dreams.

On the road to free time you will begin to notice many hidden benefits resulting from your organizational pursuits. You will begin to feel a sense of self-confidence and control over your surroundings. (Everyone likes to feel "in charge" of things!) You will experience the exhilaration of finishing the tasks you start. You will see chaos give way to order.

If you are bored and unchallenged by home management, you will especially benefit from these work simplification techniques. When you seek out better and faster ways to do your work, you will discover mental challenges (and thus, satisfactions) that will add new zest to any job. Work well done is satisfying and rewarding, but work done without skill leads to frustration and discouragement.

There are a few basic organizational principles common to any endeavor. The president of your bank and the youngster who delivers your newspaper can both benefit from the same methods. You can use them to simplify work at home and use them again at the office. Simplicity is the key.

Here are the work simplification techniques that can be used in anything you do. They can even make you a more efficient Boy Scout leader!

1. Think before you act.
2. Discard and sort.

3. Group.
4. Be motion minded.
5. Practice preventive maintenance.
6. Use your accrued benefits.

THINK BEFORE YOU ACT

This is what being organized is all about: thinking things through logically before you act.

Many people feel that by the time they've finished thinking and planning, they could have completed the job at hand. Not so! Industrial time and motion experts have estimated that workers are only 50 to 70 percent efficient. Why? Mainly because they work by habit; they act before they think.

Without realizing it, most of us are probably guilty of the same malady, and I am no exception. So many times I tell myself that there is a better way, yet I stumble along falling prey to my old, comfortable habits. For example, when I'm baking something, I know I should start with a sink full of hot, sudsy water. But, sometimes I say to myself, "Don't waste time doing that—just get busy." When baking time is over, I am faced with a counter full of dirty dishes and little energy to do them. Had I spent two minutes filling the sink, the dishes would have almost done themselves.

Why are we so slow to change? Because as long as we are making it through the day with a fair amount of success, we are satisfied with our performance.

Our daughter was involved in a regional Scout activity. They were planning a historical field trip in the city. Games, learning activities, tours and food were to be interspersed throughout the day. The event had been planned for months. However, as I drove her up to the meeting place, I knew they were off to a bad start.

Young girls were running around everywhere searching for a group of friends to hang around with during the day. One leader was frantically trying to divide the girls into color-coded groups. She was slowly filling out "Hello" badges for each girl to wear. Each girl would painstakingly spell her name so the leader would be sure to get it right. She was using the hood of a car as her desk, and at one point one of the badges stuck fast (like a bumper sticker) right to the car, in the neighborhood of the hood ornament.

Unfortunately, that inauspicious start was a harbinger of things to come. It was as if this event had just been thrown together and surprise, surprise all these girls showed up!

The *Think Before You Act* principle could have changed the whole scenario and made the event much more informative and pleasurable for everyone. Sometimes it seems easier to keep stumbling along rather than to stop and think. Many times we proceed as we have been taught, thus ignoring other alternatives as to how a job could be accomplished.

When I first set up housekeeping, I put the shoe polish where my mother had stored her shoe polish. I stored my cleaning supplies and food the same way she did. I even folded my towels as she had always folded hers. Lucky for me, Mom knew what she was doing. Had she been a bad example, I would have, unknowingly, accepted her inefficient habits as my own.

Maybe you've heard the story about a young couple who were preparing their Sunday dinner. While peeling the potatoes, the husband noticed his wife cutting the end off the ham.

"Why are you cutting the end off the ham?" he asked.

She said simply, "Because my mother always did." Their curiosity aroused, they called Mother and asked why she always cut the end off the ham. "Because my mother always did," she answered.

Getting to the bottom of the matter, they called Grandma and asked, "Why do you always cut the end off the ham?"

"Because my pan is too small!" replied Grandma.

Think before you act—even before doing routine jobs. The way you perform simple, basic tasks is usually the result of habit, not logical thought.

Until work simplification becomes second nature to you, the thinking and planning process may seem slow. You may feel you are wasting time. But remember, fifteen minutes of planning can save hours.

Over and over I prove the validity of this principle to myself. One day I was in a hurry to pick cherries. Our little boy was dressed in nice play clothes, and I didn't want to spend five minutes changing his outfit. So, I snatched him up, put him in the car and off we went.

When we got home I had to spend twenty-five minutes scrubbing dirt and cherry stains out of his clothing. Had I applied the principle of think before you act, I would have spent five minutes changing my son into old clothes and saved myself twenty-five minutes of scrubbing time!

Fyodor Dostoevsky once wrote, "It seems, in fact, as though the second half of a man's life is made up of nothing but the habits he has accumulated during the first half." That is a distressing statement, but we can alter the course of our lives with a little extra effort. We become aware of time-wasting habits when we think before we act.

DISCARD AND SORT

Of all the work simplification techniques, discard and sort is by far the most important and usually the most difficult! Even if you disregard the other five principles, using this one alone will bring immediate rewards and will simplify your life immensely. If you enjoy this type of activity, here's where you're going to have fun. If this area is a problem for you, keep reading. I'll show you how to make it as painless as possible.

Have you ever said, "There is not enough room in this house"? The problem is not your house, but your possessions — you probably have too many things. The greatest reward of uncluttering your house will be the time you save getting ready to do a job and cleaning up after the job.

From my consulting work, I have learned that those in the worst organizational state are those who have difficulty using the discard and sort technique. Let's explore some ways to make it easier.

Even before you can begin discarding and sorting, you need to determine the function of the room or area in which you are working. For example, you may say, "This is the kitchen, where I prepare and clean up meals. I serve breakfast and lunch in the kitchen. This is also where pots, pans and food are kept. Therefore, I do not want to store sheet music, broken bicycle chains or recycled shoelaces in here." This may seem simplistic, but the principle is important: Determine what function a particular area is going to serve. Then, you can begin to discard and sort.

Work in one area at a time, and keep three boxes and a large trash can with you. I call this the four-container method. One box will hold anything that belongs in another room, such as the sheet music, the bicycle chain and the recycled shoelaces. Put things to give away or sell inside the second box. The third box will hold things you're not sure of. The trash basket is there to encourage you to discard everything you possibly can.

Here are some methods (sort of variations on the theme) to help you unclutter your house. Depending upon your personality, you can choose the Fast Fix method, the Party method, or several tempting alternatives in between.

Fast Fix

This procedure is best for those folks who find themselves knee-deep in the shallow spots. Sometimes the mess gets so bad, it's hard to continue functioning. Granted, this is only a temporary solution. It will cure the symptoms, but eventually you'll have to deal with the cause.

Here's how it works: You'll need some large plastic trash bags or cardboard cartons; two large, clean plastic wastebaskets; and a container for trash. Moving along one wall at a time, deposit everything in the trash bags or cartons. Place dishes, silverware, glasses, gadgets, etc., in one of the large plastic wastebaskets. Any recognizable and fresh-smelling food goes in the other plastic wastebasket.

Use the trash container sparingly at this point. Toss in only obvious pieces of garbage, such as crumpled pieces of paper, soiled paper napkins, hard, dried-up doughnuts and empty cans. Do not—I repeat, *do not*—look for garbage. Don't look through old magazines deciding whether or not to discard them; don't eye every scrap of paper to discover its value or lack thereof. If you happen to stumble across something that shouts, *"I am trash!"* then toss it in the wastebasket. The object is to clear the area quickly.

Yes, this is going to make things hard to find, but they were probably buried anyway. Put the containers of dishes and food on the floor by the sink, or in a corner somewhere, throw out the trash, and put the remaining bags or cartons in an out-of-the-way spot.

When time permits, put away the foodstuff and wash the dishes. Then, using snatches of time if necessary, sit down with each of the bags and go through it, using the four-container method.

If clutter is interfering with your ability to function, then this system may be just what you need. It's quick and easy, and there's no turning back once it's done. It forces you into action.

Toss It, Move It

This is simply the four-container method taken one box at a time. It's sort of a nit-picking way to eliminate your clutter — slow, but great for people who don't have large blocks of time in which to work at home. Start with a trash basket, and just wander around the kitchen, poking through drawers, shelves, and cupboards, pulling out only those things you want to discard. When the discarding is completed, do the same thing again, pulling out things that don't belong. Several days later you're ready to repeat the process, ferreting out the stuff you want to sell or give away. Continue in this manner until the job is complete.

Tidbit

The tidbit method is ideal for those who can't stand to be in a mess for long or who have a tendency to give out before the job is finished. Using the basic four small containers, simply go through the kitchen one shelf at a time, one drawer at a time, one corner at a time. This, too, can be slow, but it breaks the job down into bite-sized pieces.

Prove It

This is an interesting method, to say the least, and works extremely well in the kitchen. All you do is box up everything in a given closet, cupboard or drawer. Put a date on the container. As you need things, you pilfer them from the box and put them away. Whatever remains in the box after six months is given away, sold or discarded. (I know a family who does this on a regular basis. They swear by it!)

Pile It

This method is beloved of children and isn't actually a way to get rid of the mess, but it helps you live with the mess while you're working on it. All you do is make piles. Articles of clothing, linens, etc., go in one pile or area, papers and books in another, food products in another, and dishes in another. Then attack each pile with the four-container method. This may be all the impetus you'll need to get started on your clutter reduction program.

Let's Party

The party method is perfect for those who can't part with anything. Do it with a friend or friends. It's much easier to get rid of things when you've got someone encouraging you, particularly if she has a devil-may-care attitude. She can help you decide about the value of certain items.

"An electric carmelizer?" your friend asks. "Well, who knows," you reply, "someday I just might want to make crème brulée." With no better defense than "someday I might," your own words (if not your friend's arguments) should convince you the electric carmelizer can go. Besides, if you make crème brulée at home, what new and exotic dish will you order when you go out to eat?

Since many of us curry the approval of others, friends can sometimes embarrass us into parting with stuff. When Mary uncovers your novelty cake pan collection (you know, the ones shaped like Yogi Bear, Winston Churchill, and a lunar landing module) and wonders out loud if you're brain dead, of course you'll part with them. Or maybe you'll concede to storing them in a less functional area.

Whichever method you choose, do it with the zeal of a gladiator. Initially you may experience feelings and thoughts like: "As soon as I get rid of this battery-operated self-stirring saucepan, I'll break my arm or something. Then I'll wish I had it back." It's okay to feel that way. I'm sure gladiators were scared, too. But that didn't stop them.

Discarding and sorting has a cathartic effect. Pretty soon your cold feet will warm up as you discover how fast you can find things and put them away. Trust me on this one. Get rid of your Beechwood lemon reamer, your English muffin breaker, and your baked potato stuffer, and see if I'm not a woman of my word!

As you are working in drawers, closets and cabinets, give every item a hard look and ask yourself the following questions:

1. *Do I really need this?* Fear and sentiment are probably the two main reasons you hang onto things. You're afraid you might need them someday.

To help you overcome your fear, ask yourself, "What is the worst thing that would happen if I got rid of this?" If your house would go into foreclosure, maybe you better keep whatever it is. On the other hand, if nothing drastic would happen, what are you afraid of?

If you're stashing one thing after another, chances are you won't be able to find anything when you need it anyway — so why keep it?

If you have a collection of useless articles that you're keeping purely for sentimental reasons (like the ceramic yak Aunt Maude gave you ten years ago), remember that things are only symbols of love. Can you keep the love and get rid of the symbol?

2. *How long has it been since I used it?* Things (especially clothing) deteriorate with age. Somehow they never look quite as good as when you first stored them. If you haven't used an item (other than seasonal things) for several months, you probably won't.

3. *Do I need so many?* Duplication of things is especially evident in the kitchen, but look around. Do you really need twenty bottles of nail polish, seven snow shovels, and four extra dog collars? The less you have, the less you have to take care of.

I know there are many dear souls whose hearts yearn for simplicity, but they can't force themselves to eliminate anything. To you I would say, try giving yourself a little pep talk.

Whenever I want to hold onto something I really don't need, I tell myself this: "It is selfish to keep something you are not using. There are many people who would be delighted to have these things." Since I don't like to think of myself as selfish, it works every time. Do you have a friend or favorite charity that needs something you aren't using? Or would a sale entice you? Hold a garage sale, or go to a flea market, secondhand shop or used clothing store. Maybe you can make enough money to buy something you really would use.

If you find yourself wishing for something you've given away, tell yourself it was a good investment in a clutter-free environment.

Still haven't convinced you? Set up a central storage area

WHAT TO DO WITH THE JUNK

Some charitable organizations have pick-up service, so you can call for a pick-up appointment. That way you'll avoid any tendency you may have to postpone driving to the donation site.

If you've decided to sell the castoffs, the fastest way to dispense of them is to take the items to a consignment shop. The small amount they charge to sell your things more than pays for the time, energy and advertising money you'd spend on organizing a garage sale.

If you have a quantity of things you no longer need, go ahead and have a garage sale, but enlist the help of someone who's done it before.

If you get a gift you can't use, wrap it up and give it to someone else.

where all unused things are kept. That way you will not be cluttering up potentially functional space with unnecessary junk.

If you don't have a large central storage area available, find a few hard-to-reach, out-of-the-way spots in your home where you can stash some of this stuff. Collect the things you don't use very often, and get them out of your way. The rule is—if you use something once a week (or more often) you shouldn't have to move things to find it or move things to find room to put it away.

Once the sorting process is complete, eliminate temptation by donating or selling the contents of box number two as soon as possible. (This container, you'll remember, is where you put things you definitely don't want.)

The whole idea is to get rid of the stuff as soon as possible, so you'll see results quickly. Also, quick action keeps you from changing your mind.

Take the third box, that holds things you are unsure of, and put it in a really inconvenient place. A good spot would be the highest shelf in a bedroom closet or the most spider-infested corner of your basement (or better yet, store it in a friend's basement). If something is so important to you that you'll risk life and limb to retrieve it from the box, then that item certainly belongs in your home. If the box sits undisturbed for several months, however, don't you think you can live without those things?

Above all, remember "out of sight, out of mind," and forget the saying, "Absence makes the heart grow fonder." Absence will probably make you forget.

GROUP

Whenever practical, group and store like items together. For example, have one central location for books and reading material, keep all the suitcases in one place, have one area for toys, and so on. Grouping will trim hours off your housekeeping time.

When you pick up a paperback, let's say, you know immediately where to put it. You (or whoever) won't have to waste time deciding in whose room the book belongs. If you have several books to put away, you can do it all at once without running from room to room.

When you're setting up a work center, whether in the kitchen, garage or sewing room, group things together that are used together. This is not as revolutionary as it might sound. As an example, the toothpaste is close to the toothbrushes, laundry detergent is stored close to the washing machine, the iron is near the ironing board, and an extension cord is put with portable power tools. This is just common sense and something you are probably doing already. When you're grouping things, ask yourself if each particular object is frequently used in conjunction with another.

I do a lot of baking, and whenever I wanted to whip something up I would always (without fail) round up my hand mixer and beaters, rubber scraper, mixing bowl, measuring spoons and cups. I went through this ritual several times a week for years. Finally, I put all those items in a dishpan and stored them on a shelf in my mixing center. Now, whenever I want to bake something I just slide out the dishpan, and I'm ready to go. (For those times when I'm not actually baking something, I do keep duplicates of a few of those "dishpan items" stored separately for quick use.)

The main purpose of grouping is to give everything in your home a well-defined place. If you have a family, this is paramount! Without well-defined, specific places for everything, your family will only have a vague idea of where things belong. They

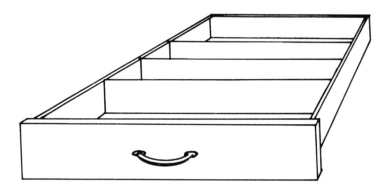

Keep your drawers clutter-free with drawer dividers

will put things back haphazardly, and you'll have to look for them when you need them. Family members need a clear vision in their minds of where things belong.

Have you noticed what a mess people can make when they're looking for something? Giving things a well-defined place makes it possible to find things before the area is in disarray.

To make the grouping principle more effective, use plenty of drawer dividers. With dividers you have well-defined, well-confined places. They help keep the system running smoothly and with less maintenance.

Use drawer dividers in every room in your home. The reason for using drawer dividers in the kitchen is obvious, but bathroom drawers and dresser drawers can greatly benefit from their use also. Use drawer dividers under sinks and on shelves as slide-out trays. You will learn specific ways to use drawer dividers throughout the course of this book.

Everything in your house should have such a well-defined place that you can find it in the dark. (The man who lived next door to us could find his socks in the dark and get the right color!) When things do not have a specific place, you become a slave. You are never in control of your house; instead, your house is in control of you.

After trying the grouping principle, a grateful student expressed the following in a letter to me: "I was one of those people who floundered for years looking for answers to the mayhem around me. I definitely wasn't born organized! But now, thanks to you, 'well-defined, well-confined' is becoming my favorite phrase!"

BE MOTION MINDED

Somewhere in most home management textbooks is a man by the name of Frederick Winslow Taylor. He was an engineer and efficiency expert who began working for the Midvale Steel Works in Philadelphia in 1878. Big deal, right? Yes! Frederick Winslow Taylor has done more to improve my homemaking skills than any other single person.

Here's how. Taylor conducted experiments to determine how men and machines could work most effectively. He was constantly on the lookout for shortcuts and ways to do things better and faster. He watched workers' hands to see if they used both efficiently and noticed that a better arrangement of tools permitted the best sequence of motion. This part of his system is called the time and motion study.

You may know certain people who spend hours doing a particular job. Yet, another might be able to do the same job just as well, but much faster. How is this possible? Efficient people are motion minded. While they are working, they are conscious of how they are working.

As I was finishing my dinner at a restaurant one evening, I was watching with interest an employee who was cleaning up a nearby table. She made three trips back and forth to that table before she was completely finished. Contrast that with another worker who discharged his duties just as well but was able to clean up and reset his tables in one trip.

The motion-minded person uses both hands effectively. During the next week, notice how many times one hand is busy while one is idle. As an example, what is your left hand doing while your right hand is brushing your teeth? You can easily be sticking things away in a bathroom drawer or medicine chest. Shoulder rests placed on telephones will free both hands for activity during phone calls.

When you're wrapping several gifts, a desk tape dispenser makes the job much easier and quicker. One hand can hold onto the package while the other dispenses the tape.

Become aware of your hands. When you unwrap something

do you ever place the wrapper on the counter, only to pick it up and throw it away later? How often do you shuffle through paperwork looking for a bill, the Post-it Note with Ed's phone number scrawled on it, or the note telling you what time to come to school for the parent-teacher conference? Be aware of your motions. Try to handle things only once.

Motion-mindedness doesn't necessarily mean moving fast. It means moving smoothly, steadily and rhythmically. Of course, moving quickly is the ideal to seek. Research shows that if you are a right-handed person, your most economical pattern of movement is from left to right. If you are left-handed, the reverse is true. Also, moving in this manner will automatically improve your rhythm and help you work more smoothly.

Here are some specific methods that will help you become motion-minded.

1. *Store things at or near the point of first use.* In other words, store things where you use them. This does not mean that you store the furniture polish on the piano. It does mean that the hot pads are stored close to the oven. Jumper cables are kept in the trunk of the car. Scissors are stored by the ball of string. A wastepaper basket is stored close to the computer.

In my more disorganized days, all of our electric extension cords were hung neatly in the garage. Because they were all grouped together in an orderly fashion, I assumed I was handling things efficiently. However, every time I sat down to sew, I had to go out to the garage and get an extension cord. When I put the machine away (you guessed it), I was back in the garage replacing the cord. Smart girl. Now there is an extension cord stored with my sewing machine.

Here's another example. We put our pencil sharpener downstairs close to our main office center. Basically, that was a sound idea. However, when the kids did their homework upstairs in the kitchen they had to run downstairs to sharpen a pencil—moaning all the way. Now, we have another pencil sharpener installed out of sight in the kitchen.

Store things at the point of first use. Here's an often overlooked application of that important rule. Every room in your home needs a trash basket. From time to time, trash piles up in every room of an average home. So, have a trash receptacle at the point of first use, one in every room.

2. *Store equipment and supplies so you can work without having to take a lot of steps.* Some people can prepare a whole meal without having to take many steps at all. Still others may walk back and forth across the kitchen many times just fixing a sandwich. (Remember, when you stand in one spot to do something, you're only messing up one spot. The more ground you cover, the more areas you are will have to clean.)

If you're already employing the preceding principles, this step will follow naturally:

3. *Strive for one-motion storage.* That means that you can open a cupboard, closet or drawer, reach in and grab what you want using only one motion. More than likely you have to move things around to get what you need. These extra motions soon add up to a lot of wasted time and energy.

Store frequently used things in such a way that they are easy to see, easy to reach and easy to grasp. As much as possible, store only like items behind each other. Avoid stacking things over two high (three maximum).

One-motion storage is most important for those things you use often. Infrequently used articles can be given two- or three-motion storage, depending on how much you use them.

Do you ever wonder why the kids don't put their clothes in the clothes hamper? Usually, the reason is twofold: First, the hamper is not always at the point of first use; and second, it takes two motions—open the lid and put the clothes in. The more motions something takes, the harder the process is to execute and enforce. Eliminate extra motions and you'll receive better cooperation—even from yourself.

This principle is most often evident in the kitchen. Be especially aware of sets of things. For example, we have a set of nesting mixing bowls that I kept nestled together on a handy shelf in the kitchen. I used the medium-sized bowl every day, and for years (literally) I'd have to lift out the small bowl (which I seldom used) to get the middle one. Finally I realized I was violating the one-motion storage principle, and I put the small bowl in a harder to reach spot. What a difference it made!

Then, there were the ice cream dishes. We had a set of twelve neatly arranged in the dish cupboard, taking up approximately 20 inches of shelf space. One day, I was wiping up the cupboard, longing for more space on these particular shelves. I looked carefully at each stored piece and decided that we only used six of those ice cream dishes with any regularity. So, I took six of the dishes and put them on an out-of-the-way shelf. That one simple act gave me 10 more inches of handy space to work with.

Find those proverbial extra hours in the day by becoming motion minded. Think before you act. Look at your working motions and equipment arrangements. Free time will mount up as you find shortcuts through better organization.

PRACTICE PREVENTIVE MAINTENANCE

Now you have your clutter under control. But what's to guarantee that in a couple of years (or sooner) you won't be right back where you were?

Here are a few ideas that will help to prevent the onslaught of junk, stuff or clutter, whatever you prefer to call it. If you follow these rules faithfully, you may well keep the problem from recurring.

1. Whenever you buy something ask yourself, "Where am I going to put it?" Make sure you have a clearly defined place in mind. Otherwise, you will bring it home and put it somewhere "for now" and the piling process will begin anew.

2. Be certain that you will really use whatever it is you are buying. If you think you'd like to have an electric egg scrambler, borrow one from a friend or relative and try it for a while to see if you'd really use it if you had one. Maybe, after all, you wouldn't.

3. Keep a running list of things you'd like to buy someday. Chances are, some items will remain on your list so long you'll realize you can live without them. Think before you buy. Your enthusiasm for a particular object often will wane.

4. Learn to say, "No, thanks." Well-meaning friends and relatives will often send their castoffs your way. Accept castoffs only if you need and will use the things you receive.

5. Ask yourself if maintaining a prospective purchase will be time consuming. If so, are you willing to spend the extra time necessary to keep the article in good condition? My mother always used to complain about ornate furniture and objets d'art

that to her were dust catchers. Today, I know just what she meant. Do you like or want something badly enough to take care of it?

6. Keep a charity and recycle box handy. Whenever you come across a castoff or other object you're not using, toss it into the box. When the box is full, donate its contents.

Do It Daily

Once in a home management class I asked each student to write down exactly what she wanted to learn during the course. The results were very revealing. As it turned out, most of them were there for the same reason: "I want to learn how to get organized so that it will stay that way!" I know of only one place where things magically stay as they are — Never-Never Land. Don't expect magic at home.

After all, you feed your family, and in four hours or so they're ready to be fed again. You comb your hair in the morning, but throughout the day, touch-ups are required. A few thousand miles after you get your car tuned up it needs another tune up. Every facet of our lives requires attention and maintenance, yet we still seek this state of euphoria where things stay organized.

Although you can never achieve this impossible goal, you can make life much easier by remembering this motto: *Do it daily*.

Home management needs daily attention. If everything in your home is returned to its proper place once a day (or a minimum of three times a week) things will indeed stay organized, and you'll keep your name out of the headlines. Daily (or frequent) attention requires less time than waiting until the situation is out of control.

Even children can enjoy the benefits of giving daily attention to home management duties. Five or ten minutes a day will keep things in pretty good shape. When we wait until Saturday and say, "Okay, you guys, clean your room!" we are usually met with groans and complaints. The children know that a room that's been neglected for a week will take an hour or two to get back to normal. However, if the do-it-daily approach is used, children enjoy the benefits of a clean room without spending a large block of time cleaning.

Maintenance can also solve the problem of "growing" work. The dishes need to be done after every meal. Washed right away, they are easier and less time-consuming to clean. You are up-lifted and feel lighthearted when they're out of the way. How-ever, if the dishes sit untouched, the job grows and grows. It takes more time and energy to clean encrusted dishes. Irritability builds, recruits are harder to find, and your mood is probably less than genial.

The laundry is another good example. Done on a regular and frequent basis, it can be handled in workable portions using small snatches of time. Putting it off causes you to spend a large block of time and creates chaos in the family.

Do it daily is the key to preventing your work from growing. You already have enough to do. Why add to it with neglect?

Another good management motto, taken from the Boy Scouts of America, is "Leave an area better than you found it." I believe that is the Scouts' Outdoor Code. It should become everyone's indoor code.

Whenever I walk into a room and see something out of place, I quickly put it away (or assign someone else to). When I open a drawer or a cupboard and see a misplaced article, I quickly put it in its proper place. It only takes a few seconds to do this. Left undone, it would take fifteen or twenty minutes to redo a drawer. It would take one to two hours to redo an entire room. Spend seconds now, and save hours later. Besides, you have more usable storage space when things are kept neat and or-derly.

Right now, I imagine you are envisioning me as a compulsive, nervous little woman who works, works, works, from dawn til dusk. On the contrary. I prevent chores from growing. Maintain-ing order is what gives me a lot of free time. After cleaning our home, we all want to protect our investment. Remember, it's much easier to stay on top than it is to catch up.

Do it daily may sound a bit overwhelming to some. But I'm not suggesting top-to-bottom housecleaning every day, just small, bare maintenance procedures that will take care of the top layer. If you can't do it daily (or can't delegate it), doing some-thing even three times a week will help. In any case, try to give your home management at least some daily attention.

USE YOUR ACCRUED BENEFITS

If you are at all involved with insurance, banking or real estate you are well aware of what accrued benefits are. Accrued means "growing" or "accumulated." An immediate benefit that grows and increases, then, is an accrued benefit.

On the baseball field an accrued benefit is a double play. The defense makes two outs when they normally would get only one.

An accrued benefit at the movies is a double feature. You pay the regular admission and see two movies instead of one.

To a coupon cutter an accrued benefit is cashing in a coupon for twice its face value. Once again, that's two for one.

Let's discover how accrued benefits can be realized at home. First of all, you need to be aware that every job has three parts: get-ready, do the job, and clean-up. Frequently, the get-ready and clean-up take more time than actually doing the job.

For example, your shirt needs a button replaced. So, you get out the sewing basket, look for the right button and thread, sew on the button and put everything away. Total time, ten minutes. The actual sewing used minimal time in this project. Ten minutes time spent on one shirt is excessive. Wouldn't it be better to invest the get-ready and clean-up in several pieces of mending rather than only one shirt?

Accrued benefits can be implemented by using one get-ready and one clean-up time to accomplish as much of a multi-item task as possible at one time: doing all the washing, all the tree pruning, all the vacuuming. With today's hectic time schedules it is sometimes impossible to come up with a chunk of time large enough to complete a whole family's wash or an entire batch of ironing (or whatever). In any case, try to get as much out of one get-ready and one clean-up as you can. You'll save time and effort in the long run.

Another way to accrue benefits is to combine the clean-up of one job with the get-ready of another. For example, after breakfast you can begin to prepare for dinner. This way you'll not only have dinner going, you'll be cleaning up dinner preparations while you're cleaning up breakfast. That's two for the price of one!

And don't forget, if you form the habit of replacing things in good condition to their rightful places, you won't have to look for them when it's time to get ready for your next job. That's more savings in time and effort.

Sometimes we procrastinate about a job because the get-ready time seems a bit too involved. This usually happens when the last clean-up was neglected or not done at all. For example, you can't vacuum until you replace the broken belt; the bathroom cleaner can is empty and you're ready to scrub the tub; you have to clean the paintbrush before you can start painting the bedroom. Get-ready will be less work if you completely finish the things you start.

When you're working on a project you can't complete in one fell swoop, and you can't (or don't want to) clean it up and put it away, try this. When you're at a logical stopping point, jot a quick note to yourself indicating what you were doing when you stopped and what to begin with when you start up again. If I was knitting a sweater, let's say, at the end of a work session, I'd just write: *Sweater back. Keep working until 7½ inches from marker.* That way if I can't pick up the knitting for a while, I don't have to waste time figuring out where I was and what to do next.

With large blocks of time virtually nonexistent these days, I use this technique a lot no matter what type of project I'm involved with: writing this book, working on a school Middle Ages festival, or making Christmas boxes for my family.

We hear a lot of talk about bad habits. But what about *good* habits? Did you ever stop to think that habits can be wonderful when they work for you? When you're preparing a meal, the habit of quickly cleaning up as you work saves the better part of an hour of after meal clean-up. Plus, you're able to enjoy the meal in a clean area.

Here's another good habit. Every day there's an avalanche of information about events that comes our way via the newspaper, memos, church bulletins and school calendars. The simple habit of noting in a planner these various times and dates saves literally hours of searching for elusive (usually buried) scraps of paper.

Problems are inevitable when it comes to keeping a household running smoothly, but you can prevent and prepare for many of them by looking for accrued benefits.

There you have it — six easy steps to simply your life: think before you act, discard and sort, group, be motion minded, practice preventive maintenance and use your accrued benefits.

Now let's look at practical applications of these principles.

CHAPTER THREE

Failing to Plan?
Planning to Fail

Does much of your day go down the drain? I used to have a lot of days like that, even when I was home all day. I'd stumble out of bed and fix breakfast. Then I'd slowly work through the house, stopping for an occasional phone call and other not-so-occasional interruptions. After lunch I'd leaf through a magazine and later get caught up with curiosity as I wondered how many cans of Beanee Weenees you could buy with $7 to win the car on *The Price Is Right*. Soon the kids would come home from school and I'd batten down the hatches and hold on until bedtime. Feeling unsatisfied, unmotivated and unfulfilled, I awaited a new day. (Do the words "get a life" come to mind?)

Then as years went by, my life changed. As a "working" woman (I know that's redundant) I was gone from home most of the day. Stumbling out of bed became leaping out of bed, directing bathroom traffic, fixing lunches, negotiating car schedules and designated drivers, gulping breakfast, and wondering what we'd fix for dinner and who would get home in time to fix it.

Almost universally, failure to feel satisfied with our performance or our circumstances can be traced to incomplete planning. Without well-laid plans to give our time direction, we stagger from one thing to the next, trying as best we can to handle whatever comes up.

So, let's begin to plan completely.

Perhaps you already use some planning methods. You probably use a calendar or appointment book at the office. Maybe you even have another one at home. If you're a list maker, more than likely you have little pieces of paper here and there: a gro-

The refrigerator is rarely the most effective organizer

cery list, plans for the high school class reunion, a reminder of an upcoming dinner party with friends. Maybe you use a spiral notebook to jot down miscellaneous tidbits, then search through every page when you need to find something. How about the refrigerator? Is it covered with notes, cartoons, announcements and messages? Or perhaps your collection is in sedimentary layers on a bulletin board and you hope nothing important gets buried.

Let's use some of the basic organizing principles we discussed in the first section. What is planning? Simply, it is thinking before you act. Planning is the process by which you coalesce your tasks into a logical pattern. The whole purpose behind this premeditation is to help you get what you want. Whether you want to buy a food processor, build a doghouse, or write a book, planning will help you reach your goal in the shortest possible time.

A PLAN WILL SET YOU FREE

Some people fall into time traps when it comes to planning. "I can handle this. No need to waste time planning," they say. Still others fear that planning takes the fun out of life. One woman told me, "Being organized is okay for some people, but I enjoy living."

A plan does not fence you in. On the contrary! It is your road map to freedom. A good plan plots the best course to follow to arrive at your desired destination. A workable plan makes it possible to reach that destination much faster and with much less effort.

To paraphrase Victor Hugo, "When disposal of time is surrendered to chance, chaos soon reigns." There are already enough crises that befall us naturally. Why add to them by failing to plan the things you *can* control?

Planning reduces worry and stress. When things are not written down, you have to keep remembering them so you won't forget. Worry can destroy concentration and lessen the enjoyment you receive from an activity. For example, if you and your friends are having dinner at a nice restaurant, you can't fully enjoy yourself if your mind is humming with things like: "Tomorrow is my mother-in-law's birthday. I can't forget to get her a gift. Don't forget to cancel the dentist appointment. It's my turn to carpool to aerobics tomorrow." When your mind is swimming you can't completely enjoy yourself.

Planning can reduce the number of interruptions that plague you. With a glance at your schedule, you can tell others when you will be available to them. They won't have to keep checking to see if "now" is a good time.

PEOPLE VS. PLANS

If you have a particular family member who always demands attention at the wrong time, check your plan. Tell that person when you will be available to read the story or mow the lawn or whatever, and follow through. I am not proposing that you become inflexi-

ble. People are more important than programs, but there are
times when you need to judge wisely between the two.

When you sense that another person has an emotional need
for your attention, forget your plans. However, there are many
times when someone is bored or just wants to socialize. In that
case, you need to decide how important your planning timetable
is to you.

When others see you write down your commitments to them,
you are letting them know you won't forget. One of our children
tends to be a "reminder" (to put it nicely). His nagging has irri-
tated me more than once. So, I started jotting down my commitments to him (get a birthday present for Benjie, ballgame on
Tuesday, money for lunch tickets Wednesday morning). Now
both of us are more relaxed. He isn't afraid I'll forget something
important, and I don't have to be interrupted by constant hints
and suggstions. Occasionally, though, he starts up with, "Don't
forget to write it down."

Here's another plus: Planning keeps your momentum going.
Whenever a job is completed, there is usually a feeling of let-
down. Checking your written plans can speed you on the way
to your next task (or pleasure), before lethargy has a chance to
set in.

Here, another basic organizing principle is evident. Without
a plan you make many "What should I do next?" decisions
throughout the day. A plan lets you decide once. That's an accrued benefit. You have one decision-making time instead of
many. You have cut down on indecision and interruptions.

To sum up, planning increases your effectiveness. It helps you
see exactly what you have done (where your time has gone) and
what is left to do. Planning helps you get the most important
things done first, yet you will still be reminded of smaller jobs
that need your attention. Daily planning is the most powerful
tool for getting control of your time. Without it you are letting
people and events control you.

You may be interested to know that next to inadequate planning, procrastination is the biggest reason for nonsuccess. So,
start planning. Like I said, it's your road map to freedom. A plan
will help you get what you want. Don't wait for success when you
can have it now!

CHAPTER FOUR

Calendars, To-Do Lists and Schedules

L et's take planning one step further by using one of the basic organizing principles: grouping. This means having one central location for things—especially lists and schedules. All the planning in the world is useless if you can't find your plans. If it takes you several minutes searching through a notebook to find your notes, sooner or later you're going to decide, "What's the use?" But don't give up yet. There's an easier way.

LIVING WITH LISTS

Many people fail to see the need for a calendar, particularly at home. I remember thinking, "Okay, I've got a calendar, and I know I should use it. But what do I write in it?" My life, at that point, didn't seem to require calendaring. I thought calendars were only for doctor's appointments, hair appointments and birthdays. If you feel the same way, you haven't seen the light. Let's explore the possibilities.

First, and foremost, you need to work from a list every single day. I know. You're pretty good at that, right? You sit down everyday and say to yourself, "What are the dumb things I gotta do today?" Then you start to write. The list is scribbled down on a scrap of paper and left on the kitchen counter or shoved in your purse as you hurry out the door. Then there's the grocery list. You're out of curry powder, catsup and dishwasher detergent. You grab a Post-it Note and jot down a reminder to pick up those items. Then you stick the note on the cupboard door. Your daughter comes home and hands you a list of things she has to take to school next week to build a satellite. You take the note and magnetize it to the front of your refrigerator. You open the newspaper and read a press release about an up-coming financial planning seminar that's going to be held downtown in a few weeks. You note the details on the back of a nearby envelope, and stick it by the phone to remind yourself to tell your friend about it.

Before you know it, you are overrun with lists and reminders. You have recipes and lists written on the back of check deposit slips, on the bottom of Kleenex boxes, and in the margin of the newspaper. The refrigerator is covered. Notes on the bulletin board are stacked club sandwich style, and there's a rubber band around your wallet to keep all the papers from falling out.

A list for this and a list for that is a bothersome method that is doomed to failure. Lists are easily lost, discarded or otherwise destroyed. Psychological theory even claims that the reason people often lose their lists is so they'll have a dandy excuse for doing nothing! Subconsciously, of course.

CALENDARING

The system that works best is calendaring. A calendar provides you with one central location for reminders. You always know where your lists are. No more searching through drawers, bulletin boards, desk spindles or what have you. Calendars also keep all the necessary information in a logical sequence, so it's all there when you need it. Your notes and reminders are presented to you right in order, all in one place. Not only do you eliminate all those ubiquitous paper scraps, but you never have to look for anything because it can only be in one place.

If it's portable, a calendar lets you review your future plans whenever and wherever time permits. Thus, planning your time becomes more useful and effective. Remember, time is your greatest natural resource. It not only deserves attention, it deserves the best equipment. A calendar (preferably an appointment or engagement book) is all you need.

USE JUST ONE CALENDAR

Combine your business, social and home calendars. After all, your mind functions as one unit. Treat it as one unit. You can't "compartmentalize" your life if you want things to mesh and run smoothly. Use one portable calendar.

When choosing your portable calendar, select one you will

enjoy using. While speaking to one particular group, I noticed that several women in the audience had engagement books with mink covers. Now there is a calendar I'm sure they enjoyed using! If your calendar is attractive to you, you will be more likely to use it.

Not only should you choose a calendar by its outward appearance, open it up and flip through it. Notice its format. Common designs are:

- *Daily*. These calendars have an entire page for every day. (Some even have two pages for each day.)
- *Weekly*. This type shows one entire week at a glance.
- *Monthly*. Here you can see one month at a glance.

Notice the layout of the calendar pages. Some are simply large squares or blocks for you to write in. Some have time increments listed like a doctor's appointment book. Some calendar pages have detailed forms with headings, such as People to See, People to Call, Correspondence, Shopping List, Daily Menu, Expenses, Mileage. If you choose this type, make sure you have something to write in each area, so you won't have a lot of wasted space.

If you're not currently using a calendar, you may have to try different styles until you learn what your preference is.

While you are checking the layout, see what else is included in the calendar. Many contain extras, such as weather maps or charts, lists of payroll deductions, descriptions of monuments in the United States, or population sizes of various cities. One calendar I saw had articles entitled "Wolves and the Wilderness," "Owning an Island," and "The Bronze Age and the Frescoes." Whatever features you choose, be sure you're not paying for a lot of things you don't want.

The most useful calendars allow you to add or remove pages. This will eliminate recopying information into a new calendar every year. Also, you can add blank paper for extra notes or other information. For this reason, I don't recommend spiral or bound notebooks.

Select a calendar that is large enough to record all the information you need, but small enough to carry with you. Then you will always know your plans. You will be able to give accurate information about your availability when it's needed. How many times have you been asked to do something and had to respond with, "Offhand, I don't know. I'll get back to you"? Keep your calendar with you, and you'll always know what you're doing and when you're doing it! Should pertinent information come your way, you'll have a central place to write it and avoid yet another floating paper scrap.

Family Calendars

The exception to the one calendar rule is the family calendar. Some families can benefit from using a family calendar, one that is large and hung in a central location. Here you indicate business trips, game times, band practices and the like. This calendar, used in addition to your personal calendar, can keep the entire family well coordinated.

Keep Control

Your calendar can help you say no when necessary. A calendar gives you an overall view of what's going on in your life. Sometimes one little request seems harmless, but viewed in relation to the total picture, it may be too much for you to handle. A calendar lets you see the overall picture and can help you stay in control.

If you're extremely busy, you may find it necessary to schedule your time off. Guard that time as if it were a doctor's appointment. Some people purposely schedule recreation. Again, they're using a calendar to help them get what they want.

Use your calendar—write notes and reminders to yourself as soon as you think of something. Make a note that you need to get new heels put on your shoes and put the shoes away. (Don't leave them sitting out as a reminder to have them fixed.) If you remember (while you're getting ready for bed) that you have to call the doctor's office tomorrow to get your test results, jot a reminder in your calendar and let your mind relax.

Put away bills and notices, and schedule an office hours session to handle paperwork. Unclutter your house and your mind by writing down the things you need to do. Read and review your plans frequently to eliminate surprises and get full benefit from your plans.

When your days begin to fill up you might notice that some of the items can be combined or coordinated. For example, you may have an appointment with your lawyer scheduled for four-thirty and a dinner party set for seven that same evening. (You need to pick up bread and dessert at the bakery before they close at six.) The baker and lawyer are in the same general area, so you can see the lawyer and stop at the bakery on the way home.

Dovetailing your errands and objectively prioritizing your tasks are facilitated when they're written on paper. You can see what needs to be done and slot things into your available time. When everything is just a swirling reminder in your head, things are forgotten, time is wasted, and your nerves are shot.

Your calendar comes in handy when you're waiting or commuting. With your calendar handy you can use this extra time to plan and review.

After you're used your calendar for several months, note which jobs you are doing over and over. What home management chores keep popping up on your to-do list? Is there another person who could fulfill that responsibility just as easily? Perhaps these are good jobs for you to delegate to a spouse or child.

What about more demanding jobs? If you need a crew for a one-time project, check with local Scout groups or church youth groups. They are frequently organizing fund raisers and are (generally) eager, fair-priced workers.

If you've put off a job that seems especially tough or looming, maybe that project could be broken down into smaller units. That enables you to advance a job in small snatches of time rather than one extended work session.

Finally, remember that things will not always run smoothly. The road to success is under construction, and no one is exempt. No matter how well you've planned there will be times when everything seems to go wrong—the car battery will go dead, someone will get sick, a friend will call and need a listening ear. Be determined to accomplish your most important goals, but be flexible. You can reschedule unfinished jobs. Sometimes you will need to dearly guard your well-laid plans. Sometimes, the interruptions are more important. Learn to tell the difference.

When faced with choices, try to decide which will accomplish the greater good. Which choice will cause more severe consequences if neglected? In any case, relax and enjoy your life. When it comes right down to it, most things are not life-or-death emergencies.

A COMPLETE SYSTEM

As a young bride, I was keenly interested in my new job of home-maker. I had a real desire to raise my level of efficiency and have our home run like a well-oiled machine. I knew how to manage an office and I wanted our home to run just as effectively. I read everything I could get my hands on and tried to absorb as much on the job training as I could. Over and over I read about calen-daring, list making, and setting priorities. I knew that if success-ful experts relied on calendars, then that is what I needed to do, too.

I went to a nearby discount store and bought my first calendar for $1.50. It was a diary type calendar, with a page for every day of the year. As soon as I brought it home, I noted birthdays, anniversaries, and other important dates on their respective pages. Then, each day I would write the things I had to do, appointments I had to keep and our dinner menu.

It all seemed so efficient, and it was, as long as I remembered to use it. For two or three weeks I was the most ardent calendar user in the world. But, after my initial enthusiasm wore off I would lapse and forget to plan my days. Weeks went by with nothing recorded.

I relied heavily on my calendar at the office; I knew its value. Why couldn't I do the same at home? Finally, after starting over many times, I developed the habit of recording my plans.

Don't let me discourage you. I hope by exposing my weak-nesses I will help you benefit from my mistakes. Using a calendar isn't that difficult, but it's a habit that needs to be developed. If you are a tough case (like I was), just keep starting over until you make it.

One other problem slowed my progress. Sometimes I would forget to look at my plans. I'd leave everything up to memory and hope for the best. Unfortunately, with my memory, that wasn't much to hope for. I would often be surprised by forgotten commitments. Oh yes, I had listed them in my calendar, but I never bothered to check my list.

Gradually my own system began to evolve. I had my calendar working really well, but I seemed to need more. So, I started carrying a small spiral notebook where I could collect motiva-tional thoughts and quotes. Here is where I kept a list of books I wanted to read and videos we wanted to rent. One section of the notebook contained reference information I needed for a church youth group I was involved with. Soon the book was spilling over with addresses and telephone numbers, a city map, a list of craft projects I wanted to make someday, and a list of gift ideas for friends and family members. As you can suppose, this method became cumbersome and violated the grouping principle. So, I decided to combine the calendar and the notebook into one complete planning notebook.

MY PERSONAL PLANNING NOTEBOOK

A purchased calendar is adequate, but if you want just a bit more, a complete planning notebook is the answer.

Many times a particular calendaring system fails to work because it seems designed for a CEO or high-powered business executive. For example, there may be designations for phone calls, mileage, businesss expenses, correspondence and so on. Some calendar pages are broken down into time increments (usually listing business hours only).

The more generic formats seem to be the most versatile. When a system is designed by you with your lifestyle in mind, it is naturally more effective and successful. The complete planning notebook gives you that advantage.

I bought a looseleaf-style calendar that held 5½" × 8½" paper. This was big enough to record in and small enough to take with me. The looseleaf style has proven its worth many times in the ensuing years. It's easy to put things in and take things out.

That flexibility has ensured the longevity of the system. As my life has changed over the past twenty years, my complete planning notebook has changed with me. It is actually the bedrock of organization and efficiency. If I had to credit one thing with getting and keeping me organized, it would unquestionably be the planning notebook.

CREATING YOUR PLANNING NOTEBOOK

Here's how my planning notebook is set up. (I'll get into details in a minute.) The basic parts of the notebook are:

1. Calendar
   A. Month-at-a-Glance
   B. Daily Pages
2. Personalized Sections — This is categorized information that

I want to have with me to refer to—even when I'm not at home.

(Note: I have in my planning notebook the monthly calendars for the current month and every month for the rest of the year. This allows me space for advance planning. However, I keep only two or three months' worth of daily pages in the book. Since we're using July as an example, I'd have the July monthly calendar in the notebook and place the July daily pages behind it. Then I'd put the August daily pages behind the August monthly calendar. Next would be the monthly calendars for the remainder of the year.

I've found that if I keep more than a few months' worth of daily pages in the book, it becomes fat, heavy, and pages start to fall out. When July is over, I'll take the July monthly and daily pages out of the book and add the daily pages for September behind the September monthly calendar.

1. The Calendar

Here's how I use it. Be sure to follow with the illustration.

The month-at-a-glance calendar. The month-at-a-glance calendar format gives a quick overview of dates, deadlines and appointments only. It's a fast at-a-glance view or index to my month. On this monthly calendar I record dates, deadlines, appointments, birthdays, anniversaries, the last time I watered the plants, when the library books are due, six-month dental check-ups and seasonal jobs we have to perform. Everything on this monthly calendar is written in abbreviated fashion because there's not much room for details. For example, on July 12 you'll see a note that says "8:30 Soc." If anyone asks us to go somewhere or do something at that date and time (or if we're making plans for the weekend), I'm immediately reminded that we have a soccer game.

Let's say someone called and asked if I could attend a meeting on July 28. I would quickly flip to the July month-at-a-glance calendar and see that I'll be out of town that day. Checking the month-at-a-glance calendar is much faster than thumbing through a bunch of daily pages.

Do you see how the month-at-a-glance calendar becomes an "index"? It's an overview of the month in a nutshell.

More detailed information about the soccer game, the business trip, or any one of the dates, deadlines, or appointments is recorded on the corresponding daily page. For example, information about the soccer game (place, refreshment assignments, directions to get there) would be recorded on the July 12 daily page. Notes about the business trip (flight information; name, address, phone number of contact person; meeting time and place; and reference materials needed) would be noted on July 28.

The Daily Page. As you can see from the illustration, the daily page has places to record a daily to-do list, appointments and notes. Let's discuss each part in detail.

The Daily To-Do List. Roll up your sleeves, we're going to tackle the daily to-do list first! Have you ever made up a list on Monday that was still good on Friday? I'm about to change all that.

A to-do list is not something you sit down and think up. A to-do list is nourished from five different sources. Five things tell you what should be on your list every day. In other words, when you sit down to make your plans, you're going to ask yourself five questions:

1. What goal can I work on today?
2. What dates, deadlines or appointments do I have to meet or advance today?
3. Is there anything on my running to-do list that I can or should do today?
4. What needs to be done around the house?
5. What must I do at work today?

OK. Hold it. I know what you're thinking. "I have things to do besides *write*! How much time do you expect me to spend on this, anyway?"

I spend an average of five minutes a day writing in my book. This system sounds much more overwhelming and demanding than it really is. Besides, imagine all the time I save by not having to look for things and not forgetting things.

Now, let's take a closer look at each question.

1. *What goal can I work on today?* Here's why you need to be concerned with goals. In her book, *How to Put More Time in Your Life*, psychologist Dr. Dru Scott said, "The fastest way to elimi-

nate depressed feelings is to take action on something that really counts."

When you're functioning as a homemaker, you're in a maintenance-related occupation. That's just the nature of homemaking. *You will never get on to the things that really count to you* unless you make yourself. It won't happen automatically. That's why we often feel discouraged, depressed and overwhelmed—because we never get on to the things that really count. I can't overstate how important it is to have at least one goal on your list—something that is achievement-oriented (as opposed to maintenance-oriented). What that goal is, is up to you: digging in the garden, reading a book, taking a bath without having anyone else in the bathroom. Whatever it is, be sure it's on the list and be sure it gets done.

2. *What dates, deadlines and appointments do I have to meet or advance today?* This is an important question, because once you list and plan for these commitments you'll be able to see how much of your day is left to work with. If you're going to be tied up in meetings all day or out of town, you won't be able to clean out your desk or restock the pantry. If you find that you have more discretionary time to work with you can go on to question number 3.

3. *Is there anything on my running to-do list that I can do or should do today? Let me explain what a running to-do list is.* Whenever I think of things I have to do, but I'm not sure when I'm going to get around to doing them, I jot them down on my running to-do list so I won't forget them. (This is just a sheet of paper that I keep in one of the personalized sections in the back of my planning notebook.)

Now, if I think of something I have to do and I know when I'm going to do it, I'll flip ahead to that day's daily calendar page and assign it to that particular date. That way, when the assigned day rolls around, the job is sitting there waiting to remind me.

For example, let's pretend next Monday is July 14. On that date, late in the afternoon, I have to call the upholsterer to get a final bid on our couch restoration. Instead of writing this reminder on the running to-do list, I'd just leaf to the July 14 daily calendar page and record the information. (You see how stress relieving this is? I can forget everything because necessary tasks just pop up in my calendar at the time they need attention.)

Date: **Saturday, July 12**

✔	To Do	Hour	Appointments
	House	8³⁰	BJ· Soccer Game
	Laundry		Boulton Elec.
	Exercise 45 mins.		
	Answer Linda's Letter		
	Type Monthly Report		
	File Receipts		
	Finish Exp. Report		
	Errands	6⁰⁰	Wedding

Notes

Steve Marsh - Sally Jones
407 Main St.

---

6 MO. DENTAL CHECK-UPS

MONTH						
SUN.	MON.	TUES.	WED.	THURS.	FRI.	SAT.
			Plants		Parade 10 AM	
		1	2	3	4	5 8³⁰ Soc. 6⁰⁰ Wed.
6	7 Call Uphols.	8 Books Due	9 2 Dr.T	10	11	12
13	14 Mom's B-Day	15	16	17	18	19
20	21	22	23	24 7 MTG.	25	26
27	28	N E W Y O R K ← →		31		
		29	30			

The daily page and the month-at-a-glance

Every day when I'm filling out my daily to-do list, I flip to my running to-do list and ask myself, "Is there anything on this list that I can or should do today?" If the answer is "Yes," then I cross it out on the running to-do list and write it on today's daily to-do list.

The running to-do list eliminates a lot of stress. Here's how. Whenever you think of something you have to do, the automatic response is that your brain clicks in and starts to remind you over and over. From that point on you can't completely relax and enjoy yourself because your brain is saying, "Don't forget you have to do that thing." Pretty soon your brain is reminding you of two things, then three things, then ten things, and you catch yourself saying, "I can't handle this." You're right, you can't handle it. Your brain is only capable of remembering so many things at once. Put those reminders on your running to-do list. You will feel an immediate sense of relief. All of the sudden your brain has the security of knowing it's not going to forget. The running to-do list will remind you.

The running to-do list also helps you minimize clutter. Let's pretend that someone brings you a lemon chiffon pie as a surprise. Great. You scarf down the pie and wash out the pie plate. But where do you put the pie plate? If you're like most folks, it's put on top of the refrigerator, on the counter, on the microwave. In any event, you usually leave it sitting out so you won't forget to return it.

Likewise, where do you put the film to be processed or the clothing to be dry cleaned? They're sitting out somewhere, aren't they, to remind someone to take them in?

We do that to ourselves all the time. We leave things sitting all over the house as visual reminders that they have to be taken care of. (Just for fun, walk through your house and count all the things that you or someone else has left out as a reminder to do something with it.)

Put all that stuff away. Get it out of sight. Just put it on your running to-do list: Return Janet's pie plate, develop the film, drop off the dry cleaning. The list will remind you. The junk and the clutter won't have to remind you anymore.

The running to-do list is the answer to the problem of "out of sight, out of mind." Things can be put out of sight, but they'll never be out of mind because they're written on the running to-do list and you're going to look at that list every single day.

The list is also a great way to keep you from overprogramming yourself. When you're working on today's to-do list, ask yourself how much time and energy you actually have to work with. Then, depending on the time available, you can choose to do one or two things listed on the running to-do list. If you discover that you have extra time in the afternoon, or whatever, you can quickly turn to your running to-do list to see if there's anything else you can check off.

If, however, you don't have enough time to finish everything you've planned for today, you can simply add those undone chores to the running to-do list. They'll be there to remind you when you actually do have the time to get to them.

Here's another advantage. The running to-do list can also serve as Plan B. Let's assume that you have your day all planned, and you're humming along as prescribed. Then, out of nowhere something comes along to change your plans. (Like the time my son's second grade teacher called me and told me Jim had chicken pox, and I had better come and get him. Or the day I planned a morning to run errands, and the car's alternator went out.) When it's not possible to follow your day's charted course, just flip to your running to-do list and ask yourself if there's anything on that list you can do.

There are also times when I'm unmotivated and wallowing in self-pity. On those days I have a hard time interesting myself in doing what I've planned. If I can't get myself going, I'll go to the running to-do list and check to see if there's anything that seems remotely attractive that I could talk myself into doing. It's funny, but sometimes accomplishing just one little job is all the impetus I need to get myself on track.

There you have the running to-do list.

4. *What needs to be done around the house?* As you contemplate various household chores, always ask yourself, "Does this job have to be done by me; or, does this job just have to be done?" Your family members, by the way, will have varying opinions on this subject.

If you need an idea to help you solicit co-workers, try this. I'll make up a list of chores that need to be done, and I'll take the list around to anyone who's warm, vertical and breathing. I'll show them the list and say, "This is what needs to be done today.

I'll dust, vacuum, and put away the laundry. Is there anything on the list you can do?" This approach seems to foster a more cooperative spirit in the family.

5. *What must I do at work today?* When you're considering employment tasks, you need to go through the previous four questions. (What business dates, deadlines and appointments do I have to meet or advance today? Is there anything on my business running to-do list that I can do or should do today? Are there any business housekeeping jobs that need to be done — cleaning out your desk, straightening the supply cupboard, cleaning up computer files.)

As you're making up your daily to-do list and answering these questions, be sure to keep in mind how much time and energy you have to work with. That way you won't overprogram yourself.

When your daily to-do list is completed, read it. If everything on your list is maintenance related, take one or two things off and add something achievement oriented. Achievement is really vital to your mental, physical and spiritual well-being.

If there is a day when there are several errands you have to run, you may want to group them together somewhere on your calendar page. That way, when you're out and about town, you can read your errands all at once (without having to scan the whole daily to-do list over and over). You can route yourself efficiently through the city, and you won't forget anything.

OK. The daily to-do list is finished. Now, let's look at the next part of the daily page.

Appointments. The appointments part of the daily page is self-explanatory. Anything with a time attached to it goes in this space.

Notes. The notes part of the daily page is extremely versatile and useful. In this section I can record mileage, business and other reimbursed expenses, or a journal entry. I can also record all information that comes to me via telephone, mail, office correspondence, church bulletins, school notices, you name it.

Let's say we get a wedding invitation in the mail. The wedding is July 12. Here's what I'd do. I'd turn to the July monthly calendar and on July 12 I'd make an abbreviated note — "6:00 Wed." (Always write things on the monthly calendar first. This becomes the index for your month.) Then, on the July 12 daily page I'd simply note who's getting married and where we have to go.

Now, we have to buy these people a present before July 12. How do I remember that? Right! I turn to my running to-do list and write, "Buy a wedding gift before July 12." Then I'd throw the wedding invitation away (unless I was saving it for a *very* sentimental reason).

Let's pretend you're teaching a class. Or maybe you're in charge of a meeting, and you're thinking of a meeting agenda. Whenever you think of something pertaining to that meeting or class, flip ahead to the date of the event, and keep the information right there on that day's page. You're never going to forget where those lesson plans are or where the meeting information is, because you always know the date of the class or the date of the meeting (or whatever). The date becomes your file reference and tells you where things are located.

Now suppose you're going on a trip on August 17. Whenever you think of something you want to take on the trip, turn to August 17 and add it to your list. (You may want to put a paper clip on that page to use as a bookmark.) When August 17 rolls around, your list is waiting for you and you're going to get off on that trip without forgetting anything.

Read the newspaper with your calendar in your hand. You should never rip events information out of the newspaper. Information about a seminar or a lecture series, baseball signups, when they're picking up the garbage after a holiday, information about the cancer screening clinics that are coming through town, a parade route—all should be written on your calendar.

Some people argue, "Why would you want to waste time re-copying that? Why not just take that wedding invitation (or whatever) and magnetize it to the front of your refrigerator?" For every floating scrap of paper (and there are hundreds generated during the course of a month), you have to do three things: (1) You have to put that paper somewhere. That takes time. (2) Clutter makes everything take longer and paper is the worst offender. Paper clutter also increases your stress because every time your eye lights on one of those papers, your brain clicks in and starts to remind you about why you kept that paper to begin with. (3) You have to find that paper—hopefully in time to do something about it.

Don't kid yourself. Those three activities (even though they're separate) take a *lot* longer than writing a few brief or cursory notes in your book. So, don't fall into the vicious trap of thinking, "I don't have time to write." You don't have time *not* to write, because writing is actually faster in the long run. But the main reason to record the information in your book is that writing is safer. When you've written something in the planning notebook you've made it a matter of permanent record. It's not subject to destruction or subject to being lost. It is permanently recorded in *one* central location.

Sometimes you'll be recording information that has no date association with it. How do you find that information? Use parentheses to refer to the daily page on which the information is recorded. You're watching TV and the gourmet du jour is whipping up a dish called Potatoes Good Woman Style. It's cheap, quick, delicious and nutritious. You have to have that recipe. If you have a recipe card handy, write it directly on the card. Chances are, however, you won't have a recipe card handy. Take your planner (which from now on will always be close by), and write the recipe on today's page. When you're finished writing the recipe, though, you can't just leave it there, because it's something you want to try someday. So, turn to your running to-do list and write, "Try recipe — July 12." You won't forget to try that recipe because you look at your running to-do list every single day. That list will actually nag you into trying that recipe. And you won't have to wonder where you put the recipe, because the list is telling you that it's found on July 12.

Take a look at the daily page calendar example. Do you see where the errands are recorded? Notice the entry that says, "errands (7-9)." What that means is that on the ninth day of July I had written down some errands I wanted to run, but something came up and I couldn't do them. I didn't want to recopy the list, so my entry is telling me to go back to July 9 and do the errands that are recorded on that page.

Summarizing then, the parentheses tell you on which date needed information is located.

Personalized Sections

Next in my planning notebook I have a collection of tabbed dividers. These categorize various information that I want to have with me to refer to—even when I'm away from home.

Here are a few of my most useful sections.

Goals

Behind this tabbed divider I keep:

• The running to-do list. I keep one list for personal goals and one for business. This is just a sheet of paper that is constantly used and referred to. Every day I add a few things and delete a few things. When the sheet is filled, I just put in a clean sheet and recopy any undone entrees from the old sheet.
   • A list of goals.
   • A list of craft projects I'd like to make someday.
   • A list of things I can do in five minutes.

Special Data

That's just a high-tech way of saying "miscellaneous." In this section you'll find:

• An exercise routine I can do when I'm out of town.
• A sheet on which I've recorded all those numbers we have to remember (battery numbers for the watches, cameras, calculators, toys, etc.; size of the slide projector bulb; size of the furnace filter; locker numbers; locker combinations; prescription numbers; Social Security numbers; clothing, sock and shoe sizes; the thickness of the Weed Wacker string; the serial number of the cable converter box—we need that number whenever we order pay-per-view).
   • Motivating thoughts and quotes.
   • Church telephone list.
   • City Map.
   • Birthday and anniversary reminder chart.
   • Gift ideas for friends and family.
• Letter page. (Whenever I think of something I want to write to one of our older, away-from-home children, I make a note. Then, I don't have to stare into space wondering what to say.)

Food

In this section I keep:

• Shopping list forms—I fill one out before going grocery shopping. The form organizes my purchases by category so I don't have to chase back and forth in the store.

- Master shopping list — This is just a categorical list of all the items we'd ever buy in a grocery store. I use this list as a memory jogger. There are many times I fill out a shopping list when I'm not home, and a quick glance down the columns of the master list reminds me of things I might otherwise forget.

Design With You in Mind

Let's stimulate your imagination and look at some creative possibilities for other sections you might want to include. Keep in mind that I am just tossing out ideas. I am in no way suggesting that you need or should use each one.

Book section. This is a convenient place to write down books and articles you want to read. When you read a good review or get a referral from a friend, you'll have a permanent place to record the information. This is also a good place to note books you'd like the children to read. Some people also use this section to list videos they want to rent. (Usually by the time a movie comes out in video, I've forgotten that I wanted to see it!)

Project section. Here's a useful place for listing things you'd like to do someday when you're in the mood. For example: knit Mother a sweater, make a quilt, refinish the desk. This is the place to write down anything that sparks your interest — a new craft, recipe or decorating idea.

As you can see, there is no kind of order or sense of urgency here. If you wake up one morning and feel like doing counted cross-stitch, you can check your project list to see if there is something you can get going on. Sometimes working with your moods can help you accomplish more than working against them.

Unfortunately, we can't always do what we want to do when we want to do it. Following your mood swings is profitable only when your mood is directly related to something that needs to be accomplished. But, when time permits, it's great to spend hours reading, scuba diving, sleeping, or whatever strikes your fancy!

Whether you're filling out this section with things to do, setting goals, or planning a long-awaited job, remember that you can eat an elephant one bite at a time. So, when listing your projects, break them into bite-size pieces and list each small job in the order it needs to be done.

For example: Make a blue jean quilt for Steven's bed

1. Gather old jeans.
2. Cut jeans into squares.
3. Buy number 16 sewing machine needle, buy yarn, buy quilt back and quilt batting.
4. Sew squares together.
5. Borrow Judy's quilt frames.
6. Tie quilt.
7. Bind quilt.

This may seem like a lot of work. It may even seem a little foolish. But the purpose is to make any project seem less formidable. Bite-size pieces are easier to swallow. Making a quilt seems like a monster looming on the horizon. But buying a sewing machine needle and yarn isn't so bad. Cutting the quilt blocks isn't too hard. Gradually and almost painlessly, you will be led to the completion of your goal.

By listing all the mini steps, you will be able to get a handle on many long overdue projects. It is important that you be able to finish one step in a single day. Long projects are easy to put off because they lack immediate rewards. Simple steps, easily completed, keep the rewards coming and keep you moving toward your goal. As you proceed from one step to another you will find there is something very motivating about crossing things off your list.

Housecleaning section. This is another helpful section for the planning notebook. Here you list your housecleaning schedule. This will be discussed in detail in the following chapter.

Purchase section. Here's a real money saver and clutter preventer. In this section you list things you'd like to have someday (a microwave, satin sheets, a filing cabinet, new kitchen shears). This section can be useful in many ways.

First, it can save you money by reducing impulse purchases. I remember years ago I wanted to buy some small dessert dishes. Oh, how I wanted those dishes! I recall how I used to imagine myself serving mouth-watering desserts in them. I quickly gave way to my determination and bought the dishes. Today, they are sitting neglected and unused on a kitchen shelf, the product of an impulsive purchase.

When you think you can't live without something, list it in your purchase section. Give your enthusiasm a chance to fade.

Maybe your mood will swing and you'll decide against it. Not only will you save money, you will save your house from more clutter.

The list in your purchase section can also motivate you to begin a savings or budget program that will allow you to pay cash for a desired article. That will also save you money. In the purchase section you may want to record the budget program you're setting up to help you save for a wanted item.

Use the purchase section to help eliminate some of life's little irritations. As an example, one of our children always had wrappers and trash lying on his dresser and stuffed in his sock drawer and any other convenient place. I decided what he needed was a trash basket in his room. I listed it in the purchase section, and as soon as I had a few extra dollars I bought one for him.

Whenever you have a little extra cash, glance down the list and see if the money could be used or saved for one of the items. If money is not given direction, it soon goes a dollar here, a dollar there with nothing to show for it.

There are other types of purchases, too. (You may want to keep these listed on a separate sheet.) Whenever you think of something (non-grocery) you need to buy, jot it down on this purchase sheet. For example, let's say you're running out of notebook paper, so you note it in the purchase section. A week or so later you go to Kmart to pick up a prescription. As soon as you walk into the store, check the purchase section to see if there's anything else (like the notebook paper) you can pick up while you're there. This eliminates those time-wasting emergency trips to the store to replace something you must have now.

Menu Selection section. This will help if you spent the first twenty years of your life wondering who you'd marry and the next twenty years wondering what to have for dinner. These menu selection sheets will be discussed in detail in one of the following chapters.

Holiday section. Here's a section that can keep you celebrating if you celebrate holidays in a big way. Whenever you see a cute decorating idea, read a delicious-sounding holiday recipe, or hear about a clever tradition, jot it down in the holiday section. If you've seen a craft pattern for something you'd like to make, note where you saw the directions. This is also a good place to note what supplies you have left over from the previous holiday (six rolls of Christmas wrapping paper, three Thanksgiving Pilgrim candles, four New Year's Eve horns). Then, when the holiday rolls around, you won't have to remember what's being stored. You will be able to purchase accurately.

In September I put a manila envelope into the holiday section. On the front of the envelope I write down the things the kids are hinting they'd like for Christmas. Then, as things are purchased I put the receipts for each product into the envelope. That way if something needs to be returned, everything is easily found. And there are no scraps of paper to keep track of.

Summer section. This is useful to the busy stay-at-home parent wondering how to get through the summer. During the winter, start making notes of various ideas: arts and crafts projects, a list of good books, vocabulary words, places to visit, educational ideas, cooking and baking projects. In late spring sit down with all your notes and start making some plans. Set aside some time each week to do a few of these things. Summer will be less frantic for you and less boring for the children when you have a few structured activities.

Odd Jobs section. Here you indicate home repairs and yard work (caulk the shower, repair wallpaper, fertilize the lawn). Nagging is quieter on paper, by the way, if you're planning to pass this list along to another family member. This is an ongoing list.

Medical History section. List names and birthdates of family members, health history, and immunization records. This section could also be used for pet records.

Personal Data section. This offers help with the many numbers we have to keep track of: Social Security numbers, bank card numbers, name of bank, type of account and account number, safety deposit number, credit card information (company name, number, expiration date, whom to notify if you lose the card), driver's license number and passport number. Other things to include might be auto information (make of car; insurance company, policy number and amount, location of policy, expiration date; license number, serial number, registration number, title number) and boat or trailer information (motor serial number, model serial number).

Insurance policies of all types could be listed. (Company name, agent's name and phone number, policy date, policy number, amount, location of policy, expiration or conversion date.)

Would a list of expiration dates on mortgages, certificates of deposits and bonds be helpful to you?

Household section. This section lists room sizes, paint colors and numbers, window and bed sizes, wallpaper swatches, etc. If you're out shopping and see something you might like for your home, you'll have all the necessary information with you. This section has obvious benefits if you've moved recently or are remodeling.

Family section. This section keeps track of sizes, measurements, and ideas for gifts. This is especially helpful with grandchildren or when other family members are living away from home.

Financial section. Record mileage, meals and other business expenses. Various household expenses are also recorded here (food and clothing expenditures, for example). Having your planning notebook with you gives you a convenient place to record this information. Jot down these expense items right on the daily squares for easy access.

Birthday section. Use a page or a half page for every month, and list all the respective birthdays. You'll never again have to transfer birthdates to your calendar.

Temporary sections. Record reminders for special or one-time events, vacation plans, including a list of things to pack; information for an upcoming business trip; plans for a special party; preparations for going away to college; wedding plans; plans for the club luncheon.

You see? Your complete planning notebook is limited only by your imagination. Begin by setting up a calendar section, and let the rest of your planning notebook evolve naturally. As you discover different things you'd like to have with you to refer to and use, add a section to your book. (Every time I stopped into the library or browsed through a bookstore, I wished I had remembered to bring the list of books I was trying to locate. Thus my book section was born.) My notebook is the glue that holds me together. I know yours will do the same for you.

And there you have it! Everything I need is always at my fingertips. As my life changes, my planning notebook changes—I just add or make different sections.

The whole purpose of management, whether in the business world or at home, is to achieve your goals. That is also the purpose of time management. You can begin to reach your goals right now by planning and calendaring. Why wait?

CHAPTER FIVE

A Schedule Made for You

Your to-do list is compiled and, rearing its ugly head, is the word — *housework*. In geometry we learn that the shortest distance between two points is a straight line. With housework, the shortest distance between two points — starting and finishing — is a housekeeping schedule.

Before we go on vacation, we decide on a destination, then we decide how we will get there and what route we will take. Scheduling your work is like planning a trip. It gives you a destination and serves as a road map for your journey. I'm sure you can appreciate the value of a vacation itinerary, but how often do you journey through your day's work without direction?

Specifically, why do you need a housework schedule? If you are a slob, you need to know that you have a task that needs to be done. You need to know that you have to start. You need to see in writing what the task is that has to be done and when. A schedule will at least help you do better than you're doing now.

If you're a perfectionist: A schedule can keep you from doing things more often than they really need to be done.

If you are neither a slob nor a perfectionist, maybe you're the "I just can't stick to a schedule" type. That's fine, but you need a schedule, too. People in this group usually fear being entrapped. If that is the case, approach your schedule like this: "I am not going to follow this schedule, but I can choose three jobs and do those." Or, "I can follow this schedule for half a day, then I'm free." Used in this way, a schedule can serve as a guide, reminding you of jobs that haven't been done for a while and helping you remember the ones that have. Once you begin to see how a schedule can bring you more free time, it will become increasingly useful to you.

And there's always the group who says: "I can see when the piano needs dusting. What do I need a schedule for?" You may very well be operating on a mental schedule without knowing it.

Schedules help you form good habits and get you into a smooth routine. With a schedule, things are kept up on a regular basis without suffering serious neglect. If you're accomplishing these ends already, you've got a schedule. It's just written in your head, not on paper. But if you find things neglected and out of control now and then, a wrtitten schedule might be in order.

VISIBLE BENEFITS

Scheduling can save a great deal of get-ready and clean-up time. For example, to set up the ironing board, heat the iron, and put everything away when finished takes about five minutes. I can iron a shirt in six minutes. So if I iron a shirt every time I need one, it will take eleven minutes for one shirt. However, if I schedule an ironing day and do all the ironing at once, I can save an enormous amount of time by doing get-ready and clean-up once instead of many times.

The total time spent ironing five shirts at one time would be as follows:

Get-ready/clean-up	five minutes
Ironing five shirts (six minutes each)	thirty minutes
Total time spent	thirty-five minutes

The total time spent ironing five shirts at different times, or as needed, would be as follows:

Get-ready/clean-up (five minutes per shirt)	twenty-five minutes
Ironing five shirts (six minutes each)	thirty minutes
Total time spent	fifty-five minutes

You can see from this example that scheduling ironing time can save a total of twenty minutes. That may not seem dramatic, until you figure that twenty minutes a week is seventeen and one-third hours a year. I can think of a lot of ways I would like to spend those hours — and setting up and taking down the ironing board is not one of them. Having and following a schedule is well worth your time. Remember, planned time means more time!

When you rely on a housekeeping schedule you don't have to stop to figure out what you're going to do next. You can keep your momentum. Stopping every so often to make decisions is time consuming and energy depleting. You conserve your energy when you cut down on indecison. You can perform routine tasks almost automatically.

A schedule keeps you from doing some jobs more often than is necessary. You don't forget a job that might go undone.

The main reason for having a housekeeping schedule is that it gives you a sense of completion. Housework is never done, but with a schedule, you can be. Monday's work can be finished, Tuesday's work completed, and so on. Even though some areas of the house are undone, you can relax and say, "That's Thursday's work." Without a schedule you always feel snowed under, trying to catch up. Enjoy the exhilarating feeling you get when something is finished.

I've been a champion for the cause of scheduled housekeeping for years, yet often I hear, "Oh, I tried your housekeeping schedule (or so-and-so's) and it just didn't work." Of course it didn't work. Schedules are very personal and individual things. They should reflect *your* lifestyle, *your* energy level, the size of *your* family, the amount of help *you* have, and how many hours *you're* able to be at home. Whenever you see a housekeeping schedule in a book or magazine, go ahead and read it, but don't accept it as if it were scripture. Notice how it is set up. Read through the list of jobs and see if it gives you any ideas. Be objective when doing this, and don't automatically conclude that there is one right method or that yours is inferior.

Schedules are sometimes set up idealistically. Make certain that your schedule has attainable goals. That way, you will have built-in success. Schedules are not carved in stone, they are written on paper. They need to be modified and changed as your life circumstances dictate. If you decide to go back to work, your schedule will need revamping. The birth of a baby will require many schedule alterations. Relax and let your schedule help you get what you want.

Sometimes a schedule becomes so involved with trivia that important jobs are overlooked. When that happens, the system ceases to function.

After a class or a seminar, people will say to me, "I am the worst organizer. I haven't scrubbed the tile grout with a toothbrush for three weeks." If your schedule calls for tedious and frequent tile grout scrubbings, then you're over concerned with trivia. Make sure priorities are built into your schedule. Here are a few guidelines. No matter the size or shape of your home, or the number of occupants, these are certain bare essentials that must be done first:

1. General pickup of the house.
2. Laundry kept current.
3. Well-balanced meals served regularly.
4. Dishes done frequently.
5. Bathrooms cleaned and straightened regularly.
6. Entry areas clean and neat. (This is to avoid embarrassment when the doorbell rings. It is not necessary for the well-being of the family, but it will help your peace of mind.)

When time is tight, just doing these basic jobs will be enough to see you through.

MAKING YOUR OWN SCHEDULE

With these directives in mind, let's make a tailor-made-for-you schedule. Simply take the following steps:

1. *Plan.* Before you can begin scheduling, determine first of all how much time you can or want to spend cleaning. Placing your schedule within certain time restrictions will keep you from over programming or from scheduling nonessentials. My schedule is set up something like this:

Monday — Clean	(two hours)
Tuesday — Maintain	(minimum time)
Wednesday — Clean	(two hours)
Thursday — Maintain	(minimal time)
Friday — Clean	(three hours)
Saturday — Maintain	(minimal time)
Sunday — Maintain	(minimal time)

How many days (or hours) do you want to clean? How many days can you maintain? Once you have a schedule "roughed in" you can begin making specific plans.

If you are employed and are out of the house for most of the day, you'll probably only have time to clean things up once a week. Then during the subsequent days you'll only have to do minimal picking up and tidying.

2. *Evaluate.* Make several photocopies of the Schedule Maker that follows. (You'll need one for every room or area in your house.) Now, go through each room deciding how often you think each job should be done: daily, weekly, monthly, or seasonally—and note your decision in the # column of the Schedule Maker. Remember, this is according to you! You may decide that many of these jobs don't need to be done at all.

3. *Schedule.* Next, decide how often you think the job needs to be done—daily, weekly, monthly, or seasonally—and note your decision by each particular job.

There is no right standard here. For example, a family with several small children and only one bathroom will need to clean the bathroom daily. A single person living in a condo with two bathrooms could easily get by with a weekly cleaning. Daily dusting may seem excessive to some and necessary to others. A very pale or dark-colored carpet will need more frequent vacuuming than a variegated carpet.

You see how a schedule needs to reflect your lifestyle and physical surroundings?

4. *Delegate.* Decide (and note) who is responsible for each specific job. After you have made these decisions, chart your plan onto a permanent list. It might be helpful to keep a copy of the schedule in a section of your planning notebook. However, some people prefer to keep their lists on index cards or large posters. Choose any method you like. The important thing is to have a system that you will use. A sample of my own housecleaning schedule can be found at the end of this chapter.

Until you have your schedule memorized, you will have to refer to your chart every day. You may want to list all your daily chores each day on your daily calendar pages. Whatever works best, try to be faithful. You will see an improvement in your house and your attitude.

I got a letter from a woman who shared with me the joy she has experienced from scheduling and getting things under control. She says, "I am no longer afraid when my mother comes

SCHEDULE MAKER
ROOM: _____

#	?		#	?	
		Pick up			Make Beds
		Dust			Launder Bedding
		Furniture			Clean Telephone
		Plants			Wash Doors
		Cords			Wash Walls
		Knick Knacks			Wash Shelves
		Blinds			Wash Cupboards
		Ledges			Wash Knick Knacks
		Frames			Wash Shower
		Water Softener			Wash Bathtub
		Water Heater			Wash Toilet
		Furnace			Wash Drawer Dividers
		Walls			Wash Hand Rails
		Cobwebs			Wash Windows
		Shelves			Iron
		Inside Piano			Mend
		Woodwork			Laundry
		Vacuum			Paperwork
		Floors			Fireplace
		Closets			Water Plants
		Furniture			Dust Plants
		Floor Edges			Shine Plants
		Register Vents			Turn Mattresses
		Under Furniture			Empty Vacuum Bag
		Mattresses			Replace Vacuum Belt
		Floors			Vacuum Dryer
		Wash Floor			Clean Washer
		Wash Under Appliances			_____
		Clean Doorknobs			_____
		Clean Light Switches			_____
		Trash Baskets, Empty			_____
		Trash Baskets, Wash			_____
		Windows			_____
		Straighten Cupboards			_____
		Straighten Closets			_____
		Straighten Shelves			_____
		Straighten Drawers			_____

In the **#** column write down the number of times a job needs to be done—
d = daily; w = weekly; m = monthly; sa = semi-annually. In the **?** column write
down the initials of the person who is assigned to do the job.

Use this as a starting point for your schedule

over! What freedom! What joy! She called and said she was coming and I panicked, as usual. I started to rush through the house, madly cleaning, but there was nothing to trim up, nothing to clean!

"The same thing happens when my doorbell rings. I no longer lock my children and myself in the bathroom in silence, waiting for the callers to leave. (Or, red-faced, let them in while kicking dirty socks out of their path.)

"Now, I can't believe I ever lived the way I did before. Thank you for sharing self-respect, pride and time — not to mention the relief to my stomach!"

MY HOUSECLEANING AND HOME MANAGEMENT SCHEDULE
Daily:

- Pick up, make beds, sweep floor, clean kitchen.
- Vacuum and dust Monday, Wednesday and Friday. As needed on Tuesday, Thursday and Saturday.
- Laundry on Monday, Wednesday, Friday and Saturday (Saturday is optional).
- Bathrooms cleaned thoroughly Monday, Wednesday and Friday. Straightened other days.

Weekly:

- Monday — laundry, iron, mend, clean fireplace (if needed).
- Tuesday — paperwork.
- Wednesday — laundry, water plants (dust plants if needed), clean telephone.
- Friday — laundry, wash sheets (and bedding as needed), wash floors, wipe doorknobs and light switches, wash front door, polish kitchen canisters and cupboards, wash trash baskets, dust and empty vacuum bag (or as needed), shop.

Monthly:

- Clean garage.
- Straighten basement.

Semiannually:

- In all rooms: Vacuum furniture, window tracks, floor edges, register vents and underneath furniture; wash windows, blinds and woodwork; dust ledges and baseboards, pictures and frames; remove cobwebs; clean decorations and light fixtures.

- Living Room: Dust inside of piano.
- Family Room: Vacuum and straighten toy closet.
- Bedrooms: Vacuum mattresses; dust and straighten shelves, straighten drawers.
- Kitchen: Vacuum sliding glass door tracks; straighten, wash and polish cupboards; clean oven hood, oven and refrigerator; clean under oven and refrigerator; straighten and clean utility closet.
- Bathrooms: Scour shower; straighten and clean drawer dividers, drawers and shelves.
- Hall and Entry: Straighten and vacuum linen closet and entry closet; wash handrails.
- Laundry room and office area: Straighten and dust shelves and closet; vacuum dryer and clean washer; clean floor as needed; vacuum water softener, furnace and water heater.
- Miscellaneous: Clean or air drapes; wash walls, ceilings and closets; polish paneling; vacuum storage area under stairs; shine plants; turn mattresses; thoroughly wash cupboards and shelves; vacuum cobwebs in basement.

Note: There are times when I don't have a block of time to get my deep cleaning schedule completed. In that event, I simply deep clean one room a week using this schedule as a guide. That way, I spend less time per day cleaning. However, it takes about ten weeks to finish the entire house. Or sometimes I only do these jobs once a year instead of semiannually.

Here's another time-saver. Washing walls takes an enormous amount of time. So, I habitually spot wash fingerprints and spills as soon as I detect them. Also, I frequently remove cobwebs. I keep very small containers of paint handy to touch up knicks in the walls. (To be honest, I can't remember the last time I actually washed the walls.)

CHAPTER SIX

Putting the Plan into Action

Wouldn't you love a great night's sleep? Do you want to wake up in the morning feeling like you're in control? Don't you relish those days when you're filled with ambition and self-confidence? Wouldn't you like to turn up your job performance a notch or two? Here's the formula: Today's success starts last night.

In the evening I go through the house and put things in order, rounding up any volunteers. I don't clean (unless I've been gone all day); I just pick up and put away. If possible, I empty the dishwasher. Mornings are so feverish, even for a stay-at-home Mom, there's just not a minute to waste. And, if you're heading out to work, it's nice to leave home without that harried, rushed feeling.

When you're fixing breakfast, everything is easy to locate. You don't have to check the drawer, the dishwasher and the sink before you locate the spatula.

There's no time for a search and rescue mission to round up the music sheets for the kids' early morning school choir practice. Everything you need is readily grabbed: the umbrella, the burgundy sweater that goes with your dress pants, the nail clippers, a comb, and a pen to sign the field trip permission slip. (Not to mention the car keys and your purse.) In other words, don't start today doing yesterday's work.

Planning tonight what you're going to do tomorrow gives you a head start. For example, if cleaning the oven is scheduled, you can soak the stove drip pans, burner rims and oven racks in an ammonia solution all night. That will save you scrubbing time in the morning.

If you're giving a presentation at work tomorrow, you can

assemble all your materials and lay out your wardrobe tonight. That way you won't be surprised by a missing button or a run in your pantyhose.

One industrious woman gets a head start by thoroughly cleaning her kitchen once a week after dinner. She says her children are usually occupied during that time and she would rather do her kitchen in the evening than use her weekends. She also says it seems like she gets herself and everyone off faster when the kitchen is clean. Another friend sets aside two hours a week to cook ahead. She prepares about five meals at a time so the kids can heat up dinner and have it ready by the time Mom and Dad get home from work.

Now that you're all set for tomorrow, you can get that good night's sleep. The advance preparation really "turns off your brain" so you can experience that peaceful, secure feeling. Ahhhhh. Sweet dreams.

GO LIKE A PRO

All too soon it's time to arise and face another day. Even though homemakers are not often treated like professionals, we need to get up and handle our jobs professionally.

When you have a job outside your home, you know the necessity of rising early and preparing for a day at work. We need this same professional approach at home. If you have a busy day planned, you might want to get up at five or six in the morning. It's amazing how much you can get done before seven. There are few, if any, interruptions.

You can do the laundry, iron, mend, file, write letters, read, exercise, plan menus, choose new recipes, note progress and update goals, do sewing and craft projects, or whatever. It's great if you can get something completed, but chances are you'll have to stop midstream and go to work. Even though I'm dog-tired at the end of the day, I'm sort of buoyed up (or at least mentally prepared) to tackle housework when I get home.

If you can't drag yourself out of bed that early, at least try to get up before your children do. Children have so much energy, and if we can get a head start on them, so much the better. When they're doing tribal dances around your bed or begging for breakfast, they are beginning to control your day. How much better to be awake and ready for them, so you'll be in control and operating on *your* terms.

If you've set aside a block of time for housework, dressing and acting the part of a housekeeping pro will help you speed through your work. Even though people on television clean house in chiffon evening dresses and washable suits, dress in loose, comfortable and appropriate clothes. Although you won't look like you're ready for a night on the town, you'll be ready for work. If you feel good about the way you look, your attitude and disposition will improve. Also, if your state congressional representative comes to the door soliciting votes, you won't have to hide your appearance by talking through a cracked open door!

Watch professionals for ideas. When people make a living doing a certain job, they usually have the tools and knowledge to work efficiently. Notice their work simplification methods. Pay attention not only to how they use their equipment, but see how it is stored. You'll get many fresh insights that will spark new ideas for use at home.

For example, have you ever seen a busboy clear a restaurant table? He loads everything into a big dishpan and heads for the kitchen. The table is completely cleaned off in one trip. We can do the same thing. When setting the table, carry everything to the table in a clean dishpan. After dinner, put everything back into the dishpan and head for the sink.

USE A UTILITY CART

Watch professionals who have jobs similar to yours. They know the best and fastest ways to do things. Here's another example: Have you ever watched hotel housekeeping employees sweep effortlessly through their duties? They have everything they need on a cart and avoid chasing back and forth for things. They move around the room in a circle and eliminate unnecessary steps. I always wanted a smaller version of a cart like that, but I had no place to store one. I didn't give up, though, because I really wanted one. Well, a simple shopping cart (sometimes called a utility cart) proved to be just right.

If you don't know what a shopping cart is (not to be confused with a grocery store shopping cart) you need to think back a few years before we were all two-car families. Remember when

With a cleaning cart it's easy to take a professional approach to housekeeping

Grandma walked to the grocery store wheeling a little cart? After shopping, she would load up her cart and walk home pushing her purchases along. We don't see these little carts much anymore, but they are still on the market.

Only a few adaptations are needed to make the cart serve as a utility cart. A dishpan or clean-up caddy sits on top to hold cleaning supplies and rags; or, hang a bucket or plastic ice cream pail on the side. Sew a large bag on one side of the cart and attach a garbage bag to the other side. Or you could purchase heavy laundry bags or use pillow cases and secure them to the sides of the cart. (Or, you can order a cleaning cart with clean-up bags from Home Management, P.O. Box 214, Cedar Rapids, IA 52406.)

Like the professional housekeeper I move systematically through the house. When I begin cleaning, I wheel the cart into a room and remove the clean-up caddy full of cleaning supplies. All the soiled laundry is put into the cart. Trash is put into one bag, and things that belong in another room are put into the second bag. When the room is cleaned, I replace the dishpan and wheel the cart into the next room.

Having a bag for misplaced articles keeps you in the room in which you're working. How many times have you left the room you were working in to put something away and said to yourself, "While I'm in this room, I'll . . ."? Before you know it, you're completely sidetracked from your original job. Also, this bag allows everything in the house to be put back where it belongs.

Before my cart days, I would frequently clean like this: enter the bedroom with cleaning supplies (if I remembered them), pick up soiled laundry, walk down the hall to the hamper, notice that towels are lying on the bathroom floor, refold towels and put them away, see a bit of mud on the floor, go to kitchen for a rag, rags are in the dryer, go downstairs to get a rag, may as well fold a batch of clothes, and so on.

Now you can see how many steps and how much time I save moving systematically. As I enter a different room, I go through the second bag and remove all the things that belong in that room, then continue as before. When my work is finished, I return the cleaning supplies to the utility closet, deposit all the laundry in the hamper and empty the trash bag. The cart completely folds up and is easily stored away.

The cart can also be used as a laundry cart. Folded clothes can be placed in the cart and wheeled from room to room as you put them away. So think like a pro and act like a pro.

Speaking of laundry carts, there's another adaptation: Use a laundry sorter as a cleaning cart. A laundry sorter is a small wheeled cart that holds a large fabric bag divided into three sections. It's made to sort three loads of laundry. It makes an ideal cleaning cart. There's a section for soiled laundry, trash, and things that belong in another room. When I'm cleaning (as opposed to just picking things up) I hang spray bottles of window cleaner and disinfectant right on the side of the cart. The cart is roomy, but fairly compact and folds up for storage.

I use the bigger utility cart on days when the house is a wreck because it holds *a lot*. The smaller laundry sorter is handier when I just need to do a quick run through and pick up.

So, what do you do if more than one person is cleaning? When we're all working together, I use a cart, and I give the kids a trash bag and a laundry basket to take into their rooms. They dump trash in the bag and laundry into the basket. When they find something that belongs in another room, they just set it outside the bedroom door. When the room is finished, they deposit the trash and take the laundry to the laundry center. Then, they take the empty basket back to their rooms. They put all the things sitting by the bedroom door into the basket and carry it from room to room to put everything away.

Now you're ready to handle any household chore that may come your way.

For an in-depth approach to housecleaning, I strongly recommend *Is There Life After Housework?*, by Don Aslett (Writer's Digest Books). Aslett's entertaining and extremely informative material is all you need for a complete how-to-clean guide!

The Tools for the Job

Below are a few of my favorite (albeit unusual) cleaning tools.

Bathroom bowl brush. Hang one on your vacuum cleaner or cleaning cart. It's the perfect tool for cleaning carpet edges. The brush effectively removes dust, fuzz, pieces of lint, and dead bugs that the vacuum sometimes misses. Because the brush has a long handle, you hardly have to bend over. The bathroom bowl brush is also good for brushing around and underneath heavy pieces of furniture (in between the times when you move the furniture). Here are some more places where a bowl brush comes in handy: on the carpet between stair posts; at the 90-degree angles of the stairs; on furniture cushions (it's good for removing pet hair); underneath furniture cushions; on cold air vents; under piano pedals; on exhaust fan grates in the bathroom. It's a great little tool and costs under $2. And here's more good news: It comes in decorator colors.

Wrist sweat band. Wear a wrist band when you're washing shower walls, windows or any vertical surface. It catches all the drips that would normally run down your arm.

Ponytail holders. These are the coated elastics used to secure ponytails. The ones that have two colorful plastic balls make ideal cord organizers. Just fold up the cord and secure it with a pony-tail holder. These holders are quick, easy to use, inexpensive, and never wear out.

Nylon net. You know nylon net makes a good scrubber for dishes, but it's also great for the laundry. If your clothes come out of the washer covered with lint, just put them into the dryer with a large piece of nylon net. The net will gently brush the lint away.

Beverage can opener (church key type). Here's a handy tool for ripping into detergent boxes (also boxes of food that are hard to open). The can opener is the fastest tool I've found for hulling strawberries. Insert the point of the can opener under the hull and pop it out. You can even use a can opener to "scrape" out the weeds in the cracks in your sidewalks or driveway.

Toaster tray. Keep your toaster sitting on a small tray (I use a microwave cake pan). That way there are no crumbs on the storage shelf or wandering around the counter.

Coffee filters. They're good for washing anything glass. They don't leave a speck of lint, and you can let them dry and use them again. I keep a stack in the bathroom for polishing mirrors and chrome. I dampen a coffee filter and use it to wipe out hair left in the sink or the bathtub. (Actually, there are so many ways to use coffee filters, I have written a booklet available from Mr. Coffee.)

Disposable sponge paintbrushes. I keep a big one by the wash-ing machine for cleaning under the lid and around the dials. For a machine that gets things clean, a washer can sure get dirty with spilled detergent, additives and dust. The sponge brushes are also good for dusting blinds and louvered doors. (I used to use a rag wrapped around a knife.) The small brushes do a good job on intricate figurines.

Magic Sliders. You've probably seen these on TV. Magic Slid-ers are wafer-thin discs that you place under the legs of heavy furniture, so you can easily slide the piece away when you want to clean under or behind it. They come in different sizes and can slide anything away as if it had wheels. They move up to 3,200 pounds without damaging floors, and they work on any kind of a surface. They're available at discount stores and are

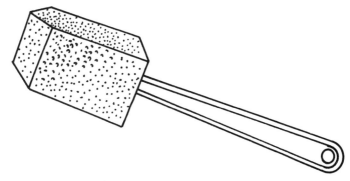

One of my favorite tools

distributed by Main Street Marketing, White Plains, New York 10606.

Denture Brush. This is a fat toothbrush. It's a sturdy tool for scrubbing small areas and is especially good for cleaning out register vents, cold air vents and window tracks.

Seam ripper. Every once in a while you have to clean out the vacuum brush. A seam ripper quickly cuts through all the thread, hair and string that gets matted and twisted around the brush.

Art gum eraser. It's good for removing black heel marks.

Long-handled car snow brush. I use one of these for brushing the dust from the refrigerator coils. (Be sure the handle on the brush is thin so it will slide under the refrigerator. Also, unplug the refrigerator before cleaning the coils.)

AN OUNCE OF PREVENTION

After investing your valuable time in a clean house, protect your investment. Avoid the tendency to be a "for now" person. "I'll just set this book on the dresser for now." Or, "You can put those things on top of the refrigerator for now." Sound familiar? The "for nows" soon become "forevers," and before you know it you're spending hours cleaning house!

Every time I go into a room, I quickly put back anything that is out of place (or I assign someone else to). When I open a drawer and see something out of place, I quickly put it in order. It only takes a few seconds to do this. Remember that it's a lot easier to stay on top than it is to catch up. After all, if you don't have time to do it right the first time, when will you have time to do it over?

Once I've cleaned, *maintaining* order is what enables me to take four days a week off. My goal is to have everything in the house put back where it belongs by the end of the day. That way nothing gets in too desperate a condition. Even though I follow a schedule and try to maintain order, I am not a slave to my house, because I stay in control of the situation.

No, there is no such thing as a house that's always clean, but you can feel a great sense of accomplishment and satisfaction in a house that's organized and well kept. Then, all those good feelings will spill over as motivation for the next day.

PART TWO

THE KITCHEN

CHAPTER SEVEN

Kitchen Sync

I f you can't find anything but your kitchen sink, then this chapter is for you. My kitchen is the hub of our home, around which our family revolves — so, it's in the kitchen where I make or break my day. Because we spend so much of our time in the kitchen, this is the place where we can save — or lose — the most time. Organizing your kitchen and your kitchen time will definitely add extra hours to your day.

In the 1950s a study was made of homemakers throughout the country. It was learned that the majority of housewives spent an average of four hours a day in the kitchen! Thank goodness for the wonders of modern technology. Today we have dishwashers, microwaves, food processors, self-cleaning ovens, self-defrosting freezers, and countless other timesaving appliances. Though science has come to our rescue with improved kitchen equipment, we can reduce kitchen hours even more by applying organizational principles to our kitchen management.

The average homemaker operates on "kitchen standard time." After making breakfast, we clean up breakfast. After lunch we clean up lunch preparations. When we bake, we clean up the baking mess.

After this exhausting ritual, we are often too tired to clean up after dinner or midnight snacks. So we go to bed and start tomorrow doing yesterday's work. Add to this the rigors of a full-time job, and the kitchen alone becomes overwhelming (not to mention the rest of the house). It's no wonder we don't enjoy housework.

Let's take the drudgery out of our kitchen work, and give it some vision. Using organizational principles, we can drastically shorten the amount of time we spend in the kitchen.

CONQUERING THE NEED TO COLLECT

Fear and sentiment are often behind our covetous feelings.
Ask yourself:
    1. Do I really need this?
    2. What would happen if I threw it away?
    3. Do I need so many?
    4. Will I care for this person any less if I give this away?

When it's time to physically organize any area, the first principle to use is "discard and sort." In the kitchen the application
of the discard and sort rules are paramount.

WHAT DOES A KITCHEN MEAN TO YOU?

First, what purpose does your kitchen currently serve? Some
kitchens are used only for food preparation and service. Others
are also family rooms for watching television, reading and doing
homework. Some homes have kitchen laundry areas. What purposes do you want your kitchen to serve? After answering this
question, you can then decide what essentials need to be handy,
so the kitchen will function in the desired manner (although you
are bound to some degree by the physical layout of the room).

For example, if your kitchen is used for homework you might
find it handy to store a dictionary, pencil sharpener, notebook
paper and erasers somewhere in the vicinity.

Take a look at your kitchen. If you're like most of us, your
kitchen is full of *things*. Well-meaning advertisers convince us of
our need for their products. Manufacturers are constantly coming up with irresistible gadgets. With the best of intentions,
friends and relatives shower us with stuff, too. More than likely,
you have an array of unmatched cheese glasses, plastic lids that
don't fit anything, whipped topping containers and margarine
tubs. And you have to rummage through a maze of meatball
makers, vegetable brushes, egg slicers, cookie cutters and pancake turners to find your favorite paring knife.

I've been duped by so many gadgets over the years. There
are multifarious devices to chop, slice, dice, mince, shred, and
dispense melted butter. Some "guns" shoot everything from cu-
cumber slices to cookie dough. Between info-mercials and

Christmastime TV commercials there's a constant onslaught of emancipating products designed to get our chores done easier and faster. It didn't take me long to discover, though, that a lot of these products ran their course in a season or two, never to be heard of again. Remember Veg-A-Matic, Kitchen Magician, the electric potato peeler and Hot Topper? If all this stuff is as wonderful as they claim, why are they standard fare at garage sales and secondhand stores? I'm a lot happier keeping things simple. Just give me a food processor and a sharp knife, and I'll follow you anywhere.

To understand what harm all this junk is doing, remember the three levels of housework: get-ready, do the job, and clean-up. Imagine that you're making a cake. To get ready, you have to get the mixing bowl and mixer, the measuring spoons and cups, the rubber spatula, cake pans and the ingredients. Then you have to grease and flour the pans and preheat the oven.

Think how much longer it takes to make a cake when you have to look for everything. First you move a network of boxes, cans and jars to find the cake mix. Then you get the mixing bowl. It's not in the cupboard, so you rummage through the dishwasher, which is still full of dirty dishes. You need to hand wash the bowl before you can use it. The next step is to put the mix into the bowl—no problem. Now, it's time to get the cooking oil that's called for in the directions. Back to the cupboard to retrieve the cooking oil. Add the oil and eggs to the mix. Add to all this the time spent on your hands and knees removing the mixer and its components from the far reaches of the cupboard.

The "doing" part of cake baking is the actual mixing of the batter and putting it into the oven. And this is the least time-consuming part.

Clean-up is putting everything away. After touring our kitchen to learn how to better organize his, one man confessed to me his method for cleaning up. When his dishwasher finishes its final cycle, he removes the silverware basket and dumps the contents into a convenient kitchen drawer. He swears his system is the fastest he's heard of. "However," he adds, "it takes twenty-five minutes to ferret out six forks to set the dinner table."

WARS WITH DRAWERS

Do you ever have to rearrange things to get all your paraphernalia to fit back into the cupboards or drawers? Think about that for a minute. Have you ever tried to shut a drawer that was so full you had to nestle everything together so the drawer would close? (The problem here is that sometimes things "un-nestle" and the drawer becomes impossible to open.) What about the pots and pans? Have you ever gone to put a kettle away and found it necessary to restack the entire set of pans? Have you ever opened a cupboard only to be met by an opened bag of powdered sugar?

Imagine how much time you would save if you could quickly put things back into a specific place, without having to think about it. When your belongings have a well-defined, well-confined place, you can put things away and get ready "automatically."

"Great," you say, "but where do I start?" The first step is to unclutter. Get down to the basics, the real necessities. Then and only then can you begin to give things a well-defined place.

UNCLUTTER YOUR DAY—WHEN IN DOUBT, THROW IT OUT

Since the kitchen is a top priority room, let's get it into shape. Remember your four-container system? Now it's time to put it into practice. For this project you need three boxes and a large trash basket. The first box holds anything that belongs in another room. This box keeps you from wandering into other parts of your house and getting sidetracked. The second box holds things to recycle—that is, things to give away or sell. The third box is for things you're unsure of. It could be called the "ambivalence box." The use for the trash basket is obvious. Use it as often as possible.

Cupboard by cupboard, drawer by drawer, go through everything in your kitchen. As you look at each bowl, each utensil, ask yourself these questions:

1. *Do I need this?* Oftentimes the answer will be "I don't know, I just have it." Is this object performing a useful service to you? If so, then you need it. Or is this article costly in terms of time, clutter and inconvenience? Then it should go.

Some appliances and gadgets are more trouble than they are worth. If you never use something because it's time-consuming to assemble or requires tedious cleaning, get it out of your kitchen. When you're pondering, remember the question is, "Do

I *need* this?" Not, "Do I *want* this?" Be sure you're separating your needs from your wants.

2. *How long has it been since I used this?* The answer to this question reveals several things. If you haven't used that platter since Aunt Ethel came for dinner two years ago—out it goes. If something is used occasionally, then it is given two-motion storage, or it can be placed in such a way that bending or stretching is necessary to reach it. The frequency of use determines the degree of accessibility.

Basically, I use this rule of thumb: If I use it more often than once a week, it gets one-motion storage. If an item is used more often than once a month, it gets two- or three-motion storage. That means I have to move something else to get to it, or that particular thing might be stored in a more inaccessible high or low spot. Now, if something is needed less than once a month, it's boxed up and usually stored in a storage area.

3. *Do I need so many?* Count the burners on your stove, and then count the number of pans you have collected. Maybe you do need all those pans occasionally, but why have all of them in a prime location? Get out all your plastic bowls and put the lids on them. How many extra lids do you have? Get out your cutlery set. How many of those knives do you use all the time? Now, check out your margarine and frosting tubs. I know you use them for leftovers. Many of you use them for homemade frozen preserves, storing individual servings of ice cream and 1,001 different things. But let's be realistic. How many leftovers do you ever have all at the same time? Why keep adding to the collection? Do you put up frozen jam every week? Then why are these containers piling up in the kitchen until next year? Store them with your other canning supplies.

Here's a painless way to set limits on your saving tendencies. Go ahead and save brown paper bags, plastic bags, margarine tubs, whipped topping containers or whatever. But, give yourself a limit. I have an organizer that holds brown paper bags. When it's full, I don't save any more until my supply is depleted. I have a dishpan full of margarine tubs and whipped topping containers. When it's chock full, I stop saving. I've found that setting these limits not only keeps me well supplied, but keeps my kitchen from being overtaken by junk.

GET TOUGH

When it comes to asking *Do I need so many?* be hard on yourself. Many people have invited me into their homes to give them some ideas on organization. The biggest problem I see is duplication. Most of us feel that if one is good, four is even better.

Sometimes it is wise to have an extra set of measuring spoons and cups, wooden spoons, or other kitchen instruments that are used repeatedly. Some things like casserole dishes and custard cups come in a set. If you're using the whole set, then having these duplicates is fine. On the other hand, if some of the casserole dishes are never used, store them out of the kitchen. If you have twelve custard cups and only need six, store the extras out of your way. Don't feel obligated to keep something in your kitchen just because it's part of a set.

It is so easy to rinse something off and use it again. You will also often find that one item can be substituted for another. One reward of this practice is more cupboard and drawer space.

Even though I do a lot of baking, I find that one set of mixing bowls works very well. Why should I clutter my cupboard and waste valuable space by storing three sets of mixing bowls? Really think through your belongings. If you can't part with something, store it in a more inconvenient place, and use your handy space for more frequently used things. You can store objects used twice a year or less in covered boxes in the basement or garage. The point is to unclutter your kitchen and make your work easier and faster.

A student of mine put this principle to the acid test. Her cupboards were bulging with mixing bowls and she resolved to do something about it. One summer morning she decided to go on a baking spree and bake a three months' supply of cookies. During the course of two days she baked over one thousand cookies using one set of mixing bowls.

"It was wonderful," she said. "The kitchen stayed so clean. It used to be a mess when I was baking. My counters were always covered with mixing bowls and debris." She had proven to herself that she could manage without all those extra mixing bowls, so out they went. She learned that getting rid of duplicates forces you to keep your equipment ready for use and eliminates a lot of extra work in the long run.

To review, questions you should ask yourself as you unclutter your kitchen are:

- Do I need this?
- How long has it been since I used it?
- Do I need so many?

These are the golden questions of organization. Once the kitchen is finished, you can use these same principles in every room of your home. By the way, if the answer to any of these questions was "I'll keep it just in case," or "It might come in handy someday," you are prone to clutter. Get rid of whatever it is.

If you simply can't decide whether or not to discard something, or if you just don't know what to do with it, put it in the ambivalence box, box number three. When the box is full, put it in an inconvenient, out-of-the-way spot. Make your possessions earn their place in your home. If you go to the outer limits to dig something out of the box, then that gadget has earned its rightful place. Use it in good health!

As soon as the "give away or sell" box is full, take it to your favorite charity. Put those things out of your house immediately, and especially, keep those things off your mind!

After spending hours sorting through the kitchen, one woman had a large box of giveaways. Then, she made her first mistake. One afternoon she spread the contents of the box all over her kitchen for her daughters and daughters-in-law to choose whatever they wanted. Seeing all those long-forgotten things made her think, "Oh, this might come in handy." Slowly all her hard work was undone.

More than likely, box number one will also be full. This container, remember, holds everything that belongs in another room. These are the things that do not help your kitchen accomplish its desired purpose: the gas bill, a missing sock, the Scrabble game, a half-knitted sweater. Take the plunge! Use the principle of discard and sort and enjoy a kitchen that's free of chaos.

CHAPTER EIGHT

Centering Your Kitchen

O nce you've pared down your kitchen belongings to a workable few, it's time to start thinking. How can you organize this essential space for convenience and efficiency? Remember, think before you act. It helps to look at your kitchen as a series of individual work centers. Generally, there is a *mixing center* where food is prepared for cooking and serving. There is a *sink center* where dishes are washed, where you get water for cooking, where vegetables are prepared, etc. You have a *cooking center* where cooking and baking are done. The *refrigeration center* is obviously for cold storage of food.

Before we discuss each center in detail, there are some general guidelines that apply. When replacing kitchen miscellany, think in terms of where something is first used rather than what the item is. We have a tendency to put all the food together, all the pans together, and all the dishes together, regardless of where we use them. But you'll save time and energy if you store things at the point of first use.

For high priority essentials, provide one-motion storage. This means you can open a cupboard or drawer, reach in and grab the item with one motion. You will also be able to replace it with one motion. Add extra motions depending on the amount of use. For example, a little-used roasting pan or cake platter can be stored on a higher or lower shelf out of your comfortable reach.

As much as possible, keep working surfaces free of decoration, gadgets and storage. This will simplify any project. Some folks claim they can work under the most adverse circumstances. But, if you're working in a mess, you're working in spite of it—not because of it.

Ideally, you should store things one layer deep. If this is impossible, store like items behind each other (e.g., one can of tomato soup behind another can of tomato soup, six salad plates behind six salad plates).

Be careful of high storage areas. It is best to keep large, lightweight items high so they can be retrieved with one motion. Using high storage points for stacked or nestled objects can be dangerous. Whenever you find it necessary to stack anything (other than plates), don't stack over two high—three maximum.

KITCHEN ARRANGEMENT

The next time you're performing a routine kitchen task (making coffee, fixing a bowl of cereal or making a sandwich) notice how you are working. Do you roam from area to area, meaning several steps are necessary to complete the job? If so, a better arrangement of tools and supplies is in order.

The structure of your kitchen may prohibit an ideal arrangement. This is often the case, so don't feel discouraged if you're stuck with a kitchen that was designed by someone who never even boiled water. Some kitchens are designed for beauty only and are completely inefficient. One woman complained to me that her husband (who was a carpenter by trade) built all her kitchen cabinets without a single drawer!

If, as in my kitchen, a perfect setup is impossible, you can work around any physical imperfections. But if you're still dismayed after reading this chapter, go through chapter seven, Kitchen Sync, again. That chapter, in addition to some of the following chapters, will give you some creative solutions to kitchen organization problems.

KITCHEN DRAWER STORAGE TIPS

Learn to think for yourself. This has been a hard lesson for me to learn. I was a real sucker for those gorgeous ads we all see in magazines showing the well-organized kitchen. I spent a lot of money on turntables, round revolving bins, dish organizers, and other little storage "space savers" only to find that some are very inefficient space wasters. Remember the only way a manufacturer can stay in business is to continually offer new items. We have to decide for ourselves whether a gadget is necessary and efficient, no matter how it's advertised.

The best way to give your utensils the well-defined places they need is to use drawer dividers. Many drawers have built-in dividers, but inexpensive plastic ones are just as effective.

Actually, I prefer the inexpensive, do-it-yourself plastic variety. Here's why. When you're using built-ins, you're restricted by a rigid system. You have to make your things fit the spaces. Using plastic individual drawer dividers (or even cardboard boxes) you can customize an arrangement that will work best for you and change things around whenever you want to. In addition, these dividers come out easily for cleaning.

Let's say you have limited drawer space, but you have at least one large, convenient drawer from which you need to get maximum use. Divide the drawer into six compartments, one for each of the following groups:

1. Two paring knives, one small serrated knife
2. Can opener and potato peeler
3. Rubber spatula, tongs, wire whisk
4. Two sets of measuring spoons
5. Mixing spoons
6. Two pancake turners

Also in this drawer is a hand mixer, beaters, and two sets of measuring cups that fit nicely into the leftover space. Other kitchen utensils not used as often can be organized in a different drawer or on a shelf. Having each utensil in its own little space enables you to grab things out of the drawer without even looking.

Use as many dividers as you need. Cramming causes disorganization. By giving everything well-defined, well-confined places you eliminate cramming.

In addition to using dividers in drawers, you can use them on shelves and under sinks as slide-out trays. Anything that is square or rectangular and hollow is a potential divider, but beware of round containers. They are genuine space wasters. To illustrate, consider this example: In a freezer, each cubic foot will hold approximately twenty-five pounds in odd-shaped or round containers. On the other hand, if the containers are square or rectangular, each cubic foot will hold forty pounds. (Keep this example in mind every time you're tempted to hang onto just one more whipped topping container.)

One secret of good time management is to develop efficient habits. If you are in the habit of reaching into a specific drawer section and grabbing your wooden spoon, then returning the spoon to the same section during clean-up, you are saving time. Multiply this time by the number of things you reach for and put back in the same place, and you'll see how those seconds add into minutes. You are reducing the time spent on get-ready and clean-up.

It seems we never have enough storage space even in the largest kitchens. Somehow, everything grows and grows until it fills the space available (and then some). These tips and those that follow will help you get more space and more time!

CONTAINED AND CONFINED

Now, here's where the fun begins! (I love to save space.) Think about the things you bring home from the store. You have plastic bags, bottles, boxes, and all shapes and sizes of containers. It's hard to store everything neatly when you're dealing with so many different entities, and the varying shapes force you to store unlike items behind each other. Sometimes you have to stack just to get everything to fit into the cupboard. One-motion storage seems impossible.

Here's how I solved the problem. The dry foods I use all the time are transferred into square, plastic freezer containers. These inexpensive little goodies are worth their weight in gold. They come in all sizes and stack easily. I print the contents of each of the containers on a piece of masking tape with a permanent, black marker. Then I put the tape on the side of the container so I can see it readily. When I want to change the contents of the container, the tape is easily removed.

Because of the uniform shapes of the containers, everything fits into the cupboard like pieces fit into a puzzle. I can see all my supplies with one glance, reach in and get what I want with one motion, and return the item with one motion.

I can find a square or rectangular container to suit my every need. Believe me, they come in all sizes. A trip to the discount or variety store will prove it. They come in sizes just big enough for a sandwich, to sizes that hold two loaves of bread. I have a separate container for chocolate chips, cornstarch, cake flour, cocoa, oatmeal, Cream of Wheat, powdered sugar, powdered milk, presweetened drink mix, marshmallows, cornmeal, pancake mix, brown sugar, rice and pasta.

Plastic containers bring benefits to your kitchen. Food stays fresher. The containers discourage pests, a particularly important consideration in some areas of the country. The containers also make it much easier to measure ingredients. You can dip in a measuring cup or spoon without spilling. But the most striking benefit is the storage space they save. Amazingly, things stored in this way take up less room than they do if they're stored in their original containers.

Using these labeled plastic containers gives all my cupboards the uniform look of organization. Whenever I open a cupboard, it seems to say, "You are in control here. You're doing such a good job!" What a boost for my self-image.

For oatmeal, pancakes, rice or whatever, cut the directions off the package and put them right into the plastic container. This only takes a few seconds, and if you always buy the same brand, just use those same directions over and over.

Here's a word of caution. When you're purchasing plastic containers, be sure the container will hold the full amount of dry food you normally buy. If you always buy a three-pound box of oatmeal, be sure your plastic container will hold the entire three pounds. Otherwise, you're going to have to store a plastic container filled with oatmeal, as well as a big, round box.

I use an ice cube bin (not an ice cube tray) to hold brown bottles of extracts and flavorings, cupcake cups, sprinkles for cookies, toothpicks, birthday candles and matches. The supply fits perfectly in the ice cube bin. Compared with storing these things on a turntable, the ice cube bin takes up half the amount of space. Nothing tips over, nothing falls off the back or gets stuck in the middle. I use the bin just as I would use a drawer. I slide it off the shelf, make my selection and slide it back. Another ice cube bin holds the blade attachments for my food processor.

A plastic drawer divider (or a child's shoe box) can hold envelopes of drink mixes, whipped topping mixes and seasoning mixes. I stand the envelopes up with the labels facing me. This way, I can flip through them and choose what I want. The divider contains them so they are easy to see, easy to grab, and easy to keep organized. If you have a large kitchen and lots of these envelopes, you can categorize them—drink mixes can be stored by the sink; salad dressing mixes, whipped topping mixes and the like can be stored in the mixing center; seasoning mixes can be stored by the stove.

In a high priority cupboard where everything is given one-motion storage, there are usually a few inches of shelf space in front of the things you have stored. This space can be put to use by mounting racks or shelves inside the cupboard door. That way every inch of space is used, and you still have one-motion storage. Small, shallow, vinyl-coated wire shelves (available at discount stores) and self-adhesive hooks provide easy-to-see, one-motion storage for everything from peanut butter to measuring cups. Wrap a piece of self-adhesive Velcro around a pen and mount another piece inside the cupboard door for an instant pen dispenser.

Herbs and spices can really be a mess to store. Using a permanent, black, felt-tip marker, I write the type of spice (usually abbreviated) on the top of the spice can or jar. Then I put the spices in a kitchen drawer in alphabetical order. When I open my spice drawer, all the names are immediately visible. I can quickly take and replace the spice I need. Putting the containers in alphabetical order makes it much easier to locate a particular spice.

If I were to store the spices in the refrigerator or on a cupboard shelf, I would put them in a plastic drawer divider large enough to hold all my spice containers. The divider would also serve as a slide-out tray. If space is at a premium, you might want to transfer spices that come in large jars into smaller spice containers. The large bottles can then be stored out of the way for use when it's time for a refill.

Another storage method is to use small blocks of wood to build little risers to hold your spices. Or, a clear plastic shoe box placed on a shelf can hold spices. When one container is needed, slide out the whole box to make your choice.

There is also available a shallow, vinyl-coated shelf (there's a three- or four-shelf unit) that is ideal for spice storage. It's lightweight and easy to mount on a wall or inside a cupboard door.

Now that we've taken care of the confusion of spice storage, let's explore one of the "centers" in the kitchen and see how these areas can be set up efficiently.

THE MIXING CENTER
Your mixing center should contain anything that helps you prepare food for service. You will need canisters of flour and sugar, baking powder, baking soda, spices, extracts, seasonings, powdered sugar, brown sugar, shortening, and whatever else you normally use when "mixing."

If you have a lot of spices you may want to categorize them and store them in two separate areas, not just your mixing center. In my cooking center by the stove, I store all the spices I regularly use when I'm cooking. In my mixing center I store those spices I mainly use for baking—cinnamon, allspice, pumpkin pie spice, cloves, nutmeg. Categorizing your spices is especially helpful if you don't have room to store everything in one place.

A bouquet of utensils provides one motion storage

I am not suggesting that all food needs to be placed in the mixing center. Some foods, such as dry cereals, crackers, chips, sugar for cereal and coffee, and non-dairy creamer do not involve preparation—they go from storage right into the dish. These foods, then, can be stored near the dishes they are served in. This is an example of storing things where they are first used rather than by category.

I don't have room in my mixing center to hold our supply of canned goods, so I store them in a hall closet that we converted into a pantry. The canned goods are used as ingredients for specific menu plans and are used sporadically. The foods I keep in the mixing center, however, are those products that serve as the basis for a variety of meals and baked goods.

In addition to foods, your mixing center should include such equipment as the mixer, food processor, measuring spoons and cups, stirring spoons, rubber scrapers or anything you deem necessary. We all have our favorite, peculiar little tools. And this center does not necessarily have to store all your utensils. The potato peeler, for example, is first used by the sink. The frying pans are first used at the stove as are the spatulas and wire whip. As you can see, if you have your mixing center between the sink and the stove, things will be much less complicated.

The point I am trying to make is that whenever it's practical, besides categorizing, store things where they are first used. Here's how I organize some of my mixing center supplies. Inside the cupboard door, I hang a set of measuring spoons and cups on self-adhesive plastic hooks for easy reach. Next to these hangs a small clipboard holding my shopping list (which, when completed, will be put into my planning notebook). I have a dishpan in the mixing center that's filled with mixing bowls, hand mixer, rubber scrapers and measuring spoons and cups. The food processor is also in my mixing center, tucked into a corner on the counter.

Where should your mixing center be? Time and motion studies have revealed that most movement occurs between the stove and the sink. The second greatest amount of action is between the mixing center and the sink. It follows that the ideal mixing center is between the cooking center and the sink, so you can combine motions, but work around whatever design is available to you. Remember, you'll need space for a variety of supplies: staples, mixes, seasonings, measuring equipment, bowls, spoons, and so on. All this equipment will be a major consideration in deciding where to set up your mixing center. Your goal is to be able to easily reach whatever you need—without taking more than one step or one pivot.

THE SINK CENTER

The sink center is the center where you spend the most time. With a little thought, you can use this area to better advantage. Again, think before you act. What kind of things are first used by the sink? Generally, vegetables like potatoes, onions and carrots are handled first at the sink. Vegetables that do not require refrigeration could be stored in bins near or under the sink. Knives and peelers for preparing these vegetables should be stored near the sink. Frequently condensed soups and other foods that require the addition of water are first used at the sink and can be kept in a nearby cupboard. A can opener should also be handy. Teakettles or saucepans used to heat water start their use at the sink. Glasses and pitchers also are frequently used first at the sink, as are colanders. Cleaning supplies can be stored under a sink: dish detergent, cleanser, automatic dishwashing detergent and scouring pads are a few examples (unless they need to be stored safely out of the reach of little children). Ideally, the dishwasher should be located close to the sink. Dish storage should be included in this center whenever practical to facilitate replacing dishes after they are cleaned.

If you're always in a hurry to get the dishwasher unloaded so you can fill it again, you'll appreciate having your dish storage convenient to the dishwasher.

The sink seems to be the central kitchen area where trash and scraps collect. This would make the sink center an ideal spot for a trash container, compactor or disposal. And with an over-the-sink cutting board, counter space can be expanded and counters kept cleaner.

The sink is such an ordinary thing. There it sits day after day. Did you ever think you would organize it? Well, that day has arrived.

Dishwashers and Dishpans—A Dynamic Duo

You might think in this age of dishwashers that the dishpan is all washed up. Not at our house. You'll be hearing a lot about dishpans from me.

In the kitchen I use a dishpan to set and clear the table. I just pile everything into the dishpan, carry it to the table or to the sink if I'm clearing, and I can make it in one trip. You'll appreciate this idea more if you count the number of times you go back and forth cleaning up after eating. The children really like having the dishpan when it comes time to set the table. I just hand it to them filled with dishes, glasses and utensils, and they get to work. If you have a large family and a dishpan just won't hold everything you need, maybe a heavy plastic kitty litter pan will work. Also, restaurant-size dishpans are available at restaurant supply stores.

In addition to my setting and clearing dishpan, I use another dishpan as a slide-out tray for cleaning supplies kept under the sink. This way my supplies don't wander around, and it gives me one-motion storage. Nothing tips over, and the shelf can't get dirty. When I need to reach something that is stored behind my supplies, I just slide out the dishpan, grab what I need, and slide the dishpan back. Everything stays organized.

If you store your cleaning potions high up out of the children's reach, they'll be awkward for you to reach and handle, but not if you put the dishpan (or clean-up caddy) filled with cleaners on the high shelf. When you want something, you'll be able to slide out the dishpan with one movement. You can choose what you want and slide it back. No more knocking things over to see what you have or to get what you want. This same method can be used for "keep out of reach" medications, and your shelves will stay clutter free.

Dishwasher Organization

Whoever invented the dishwasher gets my vote for the Nobel Peace Prize! What a boon to kitchen organization. But how do you organize your dishwasher?

For some reason, I've always hated to sort and put away silverware. I remember when I was a little girl, my mother would always tell me to eat my peas first, so I could enjoy the rest of my dinner. Well, I tried that same principle on my silverware, putting it away first, but it didn't help much. So, now when I put the silverware into the dishwasher, I put the knives in one compartment, the spoons in another, and the forks in another. (When doing this, be sure the utensils don't nestle together and prevent thorough cleaning.) Miscellaneous cooking utensils are placed in the remaining three compartments of the silverware basket. This way the silverware is sorted as soon as the dishes are done.

Since I started organizing the silverware, I feel much better about the job, and it really saves time. I'm always hurrying to get the dishes put away, because I've got another load of dirty dishes to put in. I've noticed also that frequently when I'm preparing food, the gadget or dish I need is in the dishwasher. When I always put things into the dishwasher in the same general area, I can reach in fast and grab what I need.

Remember that a dishwasher can wash things other than dishes. Decorative glass from lights, figurines, toothbrushes, combs and brushes (remove excess hair first), exhaust filters, baseball caps and furnace register vents, to name a few, can easily be tackled and cleaned in the dishwasher. In the case of the furnace vents, you might want to rinse them in the sink first. If they have been long neglected, they may need a few swipes with a scrub brush. So many times I have cut my knuckles to pieces scrubbing those vents with a toothbrush. Never again. This way, my dishwasher can do all the vents in my house while I do something else.

One word of caution—dishwasher detergents and heat might remove paint from some objects, and you must be careful not to put in anything that will break or melt.

Here are my favorite dishwasher hints. Put a plastic scrubber or piece of plastic canvas in one of the compartments of the silverware basket. That will keep things like corn holders, small lids and utensils from falling through the basket. Yet, the soap and water can easily pass through to clean and rinse the items. (Some people put these small, lightweight things in a mesh bag before they put them into the dishwasher.)

How many times have you opened the dishwasher and wondered if the dishes were clean or dirty? Whenever you empty the dishwasher, fill up the soap dishes and close the little trap door. When you open the dishwasher and see the soap dish closed, you'll know the dishes need cleaning. Another idea is to put a small glass or cup right side up on the top shelf of the dishwasher. When the cup is holding water, you know the dishes have been cleaned.

What if you don't have a dishwasher? Is there any way to

keep from having a kitchen full of dirty dishes? I would keep a dishpan, kitty litter pan, or vinyl wastebasket under my kitchen sink and use it to hold my rinsed, dirty dishes. This would certainly eliminate the untidiness of accumulated dishes and may also prevent you from having to wash dishes so often.

As your troubles go down the drain, let's move from the sink to another kitchen center.

THE REFRIGERATOR CENTER

Open your refrigerator door and take in the view. Do you have jars and bottles scattered here and there? Are there any foreign-looking objects needing attention? How about the crisper, and what is the state of the vegetables therein? Remember, celery is supposed to be firm and crisp. Tomatoes are supposed to be totally red with no black spots or fur of any kind. If the view in your refrigerator is less than breathtaking, read on.

As I've said, home management experts tell us to have a place for everything and have everything in its place. It's hard to apply this advice to the refrigerator, though. It's such a great catchall; just open the door and start shoving things in. This is why the advice of our home management expert is so important.

First, have a place for everything. It's much easier than it sounds. Designate areas of your refrigerator for certain purposes. For example, the top shelf of our refrigerator holds dairy products and beverages. The second shelf holds anything that needs to be used within a short period of time. This is where all leftovers reside.

On the bottom shelf a plastic bread storage box (without the lid) is a handy slide-out tray holding cheese and lunch meat. Also on the bottom shelf, a large, square plastic container holds all the bottles and jars that would otherwise find their way into a dark corner. I simply slide out the tray, make my selection, and slide the tray back. Give your miscellaneous jars and bottles a well-defined place and watch your organized refrigerator take shape.

Bottles of baby formula can also be stored in a tray or soft drink carton so they can be moved around as a single unit. Difficult things, like watermelon, can be stored more easily if a shower cap is placed over the cut end. If you have sandwiches or hamburgers often, place all the sandwich fixings (catsup, mustard, relish, mayo, pickles, luncheon meat and cheese) in a container and slide out the whole tray with one motion. Set it on the table and you're ready to go.

The storage on the door is convenient for one-motion storage of condiments that you use all the time. If your refrigerator is several steps from your cooking area, an ice cube bin holds about three and a half dozen eggs and can be a real step-saving container. A bin can also hold a few pounds of margarine and allow you to grab a new stick quickly. The same bins make good organizers for the refrigerator freezer. I have one to hold leftover meat and one for leftover vegetables.

In the refrigerator, leftovers can cause a real congestion problem. Whenever possible, store them in see-through containers. Leftovers stored in this way will be easier to remember. To save precious space, use square or rectangular containers. And when making your meal plans, don't forget the leftovers. That will also cut down on a refrigerator congestion problem.

The Cold War Is Over

The best way I know to organize the deep freeze is to use heavy cardboard boxes. Use one box for pork and ham, one for roasts, one for steaks, etc. Of course, freezer baskets are available at a cost, and square bicycle baskets are another possibility.

In a chest-type freezer, the boxes (with or without the tops) can be stacked, allowing you to use every inch of freezer space to the best possible advantage. When the freezer is full, a map of the freezer can help you locate the needed food quickly.

With an upright freezer, simply measure the depth, width and height of the area between shelves. Then find some heavy cardboard cartons that will fit into the existing spaces, and you'll have instant drawers. Cut a small half circle in the front of each box to serve as a handle and enable you to pull out the drawers and make your selection. Be sure the box fronts are well labeled, so you'll know what's inside.

Now, let's go one step further with freezer efficiency. I have a perpetual freezer inventory on a sheet of graph paper hanging inside a kitchen cupboard door. On the left side of the sheet I have listed, in alphabetical order, all the things we usually have in our freezer. The vertical columns on the graph paper are numbered along the top and bottom. Then, beside each listed item, I check off the number on hand of that particular food. As I remove something from the freezer, I make an *X* through the check mark, starting at the right side of the graph paper and working to the left as things are used. I am then able to see how many packages of each category are left.

This same type of inventory chart is good for any things you have stored. It can be used for keeping a record of your home preserved food. It will also give you a better idea of how much food to preserve next year. I increase the life of my chart by making the checks and *X*s in pencil. This way, when food is re-placed, I can erase the previous markings and indicate the amount currently on hand. I also reinforce the margins of the chart with transparent tape (the kind you can write on).

Now you can open your refrigerator or freezer, stand back and take in the view. Breathtaking, isn't it?

THE COOKING CENTER

At the stove you use pots and pans, lids, griddles, spoons for stirring, hot pads, tongs and a can opener.

Items used in this center are things like cooking oil, canned vegetables and other foods you pour directly into the pan, vege-table coating spray, salt, pepper and other seasonings.

Obviously, a cooking center and mixing center right next to each other will prevent your needing duplicate items at each (for example, a can opener by the stove and one in the mixing cen-ter). Currently, my mixing center is located next to the sink, but across from the cooking center. The cooking center is just a pivot and a step away, so I don't duplicate things. In other words, don't make setting up your centers a big deal.

If you have a number of pans, choose four of the most versatile (or the ones you use all of the time) and store them in the cooking center. Put the remaining pans in another cupboard. You won't need them often enough to worry about their accessibility.

Don't store pots and pans in the oven itself. Not only is this practice a fire hazard, it can be hard on your pans if you forget they're inside and turn on the self-cleaning oven. And the added inconvenience of removing the pans every time you want to bake something makes oven storage a most undesirable practice.

Pans are frequently stored on a cupboard shelf, but a deep drawer might also work if that's all you have available. I use a plastic bread container (the one-loaf size) without the lid to hold my pot and pan lids. The container slides out from the shelf so I can choose the lid I want. The lids are standing up and are well contained, not piled in a drawer or sliding around the cupboard.

Make a handy slide-out tray for pot and pan lids by standing them in a plastic container

To further simplify this particular storage problem, mark (with permanent marker) the bottom of each plastic container with a symbol, letter or number. Mark its respective lid with the same symbol, letter or number. Then when you use a container, you can easily find the right lid.

Have you ever opened a cupboard and been met by an oncoming frying pan or a barrage of lids? Then you know what I mean. There are also commercial products available especially designed to hold lids for pots and pans. Before buying one, though, make sure all your lids will fit into it.

Hanging storage for cooking vessels and utensils is the method used in most restaurants and other commercial kitchens. For home use, though, think about the extra cleaning you'll have to do to keep it all picture perfect. Also, anything hanging near a cooking center is subject to splatters and grease film. With any system you choose, ask yourself if it's worth the time it's going to take to maintain.

Keep a stack of coffee filters close to the cooking center. They make handy, disposable spoon rests. (A dampened sponge works well, too.) Also, place a few coffee filters between nesting non-stick pans to keep them from getting scratched.

Baking pans can be stored in the cooking or mixing center, but most of us just have to settle for whatever spot is big enough to hold them. Lots of kitchens have built-in dividers for vertical storage of things like baking sheets. I don't have a built-in organizer, so I improvised. I went to a discount store and bought a vertical letter tray in the office department. (This is the kind of tray you might find on a secretary's desk.) This tray is 13 inches wide and has six vertical compartments. I put this tray on a cupboard shelf and it neatly holds and organizes two 9″ × 9″ pans, two wire racks, six pie pans, five cake pans, and four muffin tins. I can slide out just the pan I want without disturbing anything else.

Now that we've covered all the centers, use these tips as a guide to help you arrive at the very best arrangement for you. Keep looking for better and faster ways to do things. Notice where things are first used and store them at that point. As solutions unfold, you will wonder why you didn't do this years before. Don't waste any more time. See if a better working arrangement will save wear and tear on you and your kitchen!

CHAPTER NINE

Curing Mealtime Madness

I spent the first twenty years of my life wondering who I would marry. I spent the next twenty years wondering what I should fix for dinner. That plaintive cry (usually heard at 4:30 in the afternoon) has caused more panic than the stock market crash. With mealtime minutes away, dread and terror strike. We scramble here and there scrounging up a miscellany of foods to throw on the table.

No matter what my day has been like, the atmosphere at mealtime is not usually conducive to leisurely poring through my Julia Child cookbook. While it's not easy to serve a well-balanced, nutritious meal without slaving away in a hot kitchen, there are a few strategies that help me cope with hectic dinner hours. Let's begin at the beginning of any meal — recipes.

ARE YOU FILING OR PILING RECIPES?

I'll bet somewhere in your house there is a box, drawer or basket stuffed with recipes you're going to try someday. These are the very recipes that are going to make you the next mega-hit of the potluck supper, right?

Maybe that new brownie recipe you saw is better than the one you're using now. After all, we can't make second-rate brownies, can we? They have to be the best. There's a little one-upmanship in all of us when it comes to baking.

Searching for and saving new recipes is a wonderful boon to menu planning and good eating *only* if the recipes are used. You've probably told yourself time and time again that someday soon you'll sort through your collection and discover some culinary gems. And you're still waiting for that great and glorious day when you will spend hours digging through your collection trying to ferret out something new to try.

A good recipe filing system allows you to clip and save to your heart's content. It also makes the recipes easy to find, which makes them more usable. Here's the method I use: I purchased a Rolodex file that holds five hundred 3" × 5" cards. Then, I made labels such as: appetizers, beverages, bread, breakfast, desserts, main dishes and side dishes. I put these labels over the *A-B-C-D* Rolodex alphabet guides. Now our recipes are filed behind each category in alphabetical order. I use this file only for the recipes that are tried and true. I don't clutter it up with recipes we haven't tried. This is the best way I've found to store and use recipes. The card file stays open (you never lose your place) and you can read the recipe while it's filed. The cards never become disorganized, because the recipes never leave the card file.

The card file can lead you to the page of a cookbook, too. For example, if you don't want to copy down the recipe for Swiss steak, make a recipe card that says Swiss steak. Under the heading write the name of the book and the page number where the recipe can be found, such as: *Hearty Main Dishes*, page 28. This helps if you have a lot of cookbooks and can't remember which book a particular recipe is in.

Transferring your recipes to the cards doesn't have to be a gut-wrenching job. As soon as you select a recipe to use, take just a minute (and that's really all it takes) and write it on a Rolodex card. This is a gradual and painless way to get the job done. I still make this a practice. If I get a recipe out of one of my cookbooks, I quickly copy it onto a card. It's so nice to have every recipe I need in *one* place.

Now, what about all those recipes I rip out of magazines and newspapers? What about that great dessert I had at church and the appetizer I was served at the Tupperware party? Whatever system you use, don't write recipes in the margin around the newspaper, on the bottom of a Kleenex box, or on the back of the ever-popular check deposit slip. I keep a few Rolodex cards right in my planning notebook. That way, if I'm in a doctor's office and see a great recipe in a magazine, I have a card to write it on. Ditto if I get a new recipe. I just jot it on the card and snap it into the file as soon as I get home.

Okay. That takes care of some of the recipes, but what about the rest of them?

I got several letter-size folders and gave them these headings: appetizers, beverages, breads, breakfast, cakes, frostings/fillings, candy, canning and freezing, cookies, desserts, diets, holidays, main dishes, vegetables and salads. The folders fit nicely into a large shoe box. When I see a recipe I'd like to try, I tear it out (when possible) or photocopy it, and file it in the proper file folder. Then, when the recipe is tried and enjoyed, I file it in the card file. (Whenever I can, I staple or glue the original recipe onto the file card. Otherwise, I hand copy it or type it on the file card.) If we didn't like the recipe, I just toss it away.

Frequently, you'll find recipes for a meat dish, beverage and dessert all on the same page. What then? Spend the few seconds it will take to cut the recipes apart. It will increase the likelihood that you'll use the recipe. Most of us have a bevy of booklets — recipes for sweetened condensed milk, Jell-O instant pudding, cake decorating, cream cheese, Bisquick, and the *Family Circle* nutrition and calorie counter. They come unasked for in the mail. We send in for them or rip them out of magazines. They're hard to store, because they come in so many different sizes and paper weights. They're not very sturdy. To control all of this spillage, I bought a tagboard single-pocket expanding file and put all the booklets inside. The file sits on the shelf next to the rest of my cookbooks. It keeps everything contained, yet easy to find, and it looks nice.

If you are a cookbook collector, try to keep handy only the cookbooks you use all the time. I have my basic cookbooks in the kitchen. The others are on the bookshelves with the other books. I can easily get to them and use them, but they aren't wasting valuable kitchen space.

My friend Marilyn is one of the best cooks I know. Here's an idea she shared with me. When she clips out a recipe, she dates it and puts it on the front of the refrigerator. If she doesn't try the recipe within ten days, she throws it out. Not wanting to take a chance on losing a great recipe, she usually makes it. I know this is the secret behind her culinary success. She has such a large repertoire that everyone I know wants her to feed them!

So, if you're still collecting one delicious-sounding recipe after another (and you already have 659 untried recipes piled up somewhere), tell yourself that you are saving—not cooking. You're becoming a better recipe clipper, not a better cook. Don't waste time clipping—start filing and cooking!

PLANNING THE MEAL

When planning a meal, start with the first basic organizing principle: Think before you act. When applied specifically to meals, this principle means planning menus.

Every meal you serve should fulfill four goals:

1. The meal should be nutritious.
2. The meal should fit into an established food budget.
3. The meal should please the family.
4. The meal should fit your time and energy limits.

Careful meal planning can reduce mealtime madness and assure the realization of these four basic goals.

Goal Number One: Good Nutrition

Volumes have been written on the subject of nutrition. It is the theme of countless newspaper and magazine articles. As science unfolds the mysteries of various diseases and ailments, we have become progressively more aware of the importance of nutrition. I am not qualified, nor would space permit me, to adequately cover the subject, but I can say for a fact that planning menus will improve the nutritional value of your meals.

Here's how. When meals are left to chance, and we throw together whatever we can find, we're usually thinking only of goal number three (the meal should please the family). My general thinking on days like this is, "Right now I've just got to get everyone fed and satisfied. I'll serve peas and carrots tomorrow." (I always promise myself I'll do better tomorrow.) Planning helps me focus on the other goals as well.

When meal plans are recorded, you can almost see what you're going to serve, so bad combinations are easier to detect. For example, if your meal plans are only in your mind you may not realize that you are about to serve a pineapple fruit cup, a Jell-O fruit salad and strawberry pie at the same meal. On paper the mistake is obvious.

You may also notice that you've duplicated ingredients in a casserole and salad—macaroni salad served with pasta, for example. You will have an overview of how the food is being prepared. For instance, fried potatoes, fried chicken and fried eggplant indicate that all courses are fried. From a nutritional standpoint we don't need to eat so many fried foods. Also, preparing everything in the same fashion eliminates the variety needed for palatable meals. A menu including creamed potatoes, Harvard beets and cottage pudding gives you a meal with too many sauces. It's easier to visualize your meal when your plans are written. Sometimes you'll "see" too much of one color.

From the first grade we've been taught about the four basic food groups: the meat group, the milk group, the fruit and vegetable group, and the whole grain, enriched or restored cereals group. Today we're schooled in the food pyramid, which shows us in what quantities the basic four should be consumed. More than ever before we have a wealth of nutritional information at our fingertips. By putting this knowledge to use we can lead stronger, healthier and longer lives.

Goal Number Two: Meals Within the Budget

There are a number of ways in which meal planning will help you stay within a given food budget. If your family sits down to a real groaning board on Monday night, you can compensate with less expensive meals on Tuesday and Thursday. You have control over the menu and the cost of the meal because of planning.

Having meal ideas recorded lets you shop from a specific list, lessening the number of impulse purchases (which, by the way, are a major source of overspending). With firm plans in mind, you can take advantage of coupons and advertised and in-season specials. Left to chance, meals require extra trips to the market to fill in missing ingredients. Staying out of the stores is one of the best methods for saving money, because every visit tempts us to buy extras that unnecessarily eat up the food budget.

Frantic, thrown-together meals often include costly convenience foods that take yet another bite out of the food budget. And it's mealtime madness that drives many of us to fast-food restaurants. These occasional treats are a nice, but costly diversion. With scheduled meal plans you manage your food preparation time better, so convenience foods are not necessary. And with meal plans you can also include leftovers and cut down on waste.

Goal Number Three: Meals That Please the Family

If there were no other goal but this, the meal manager would have an easy job. But combined with the other goals, this becomes increasingly difficult to achieve. Add to that the likes and dislikes within any given family and you have what seems to be insurmountable odds. Sometimes it's a real coup to have meals eaten without complaint and with real enjoyment! Once again, meal planning can help.

If you were to ask a thousand people, "What makes a meal pleasing?" you would get hundreds of different answers. But the responses would probably fall into three main areas:

1. It has to please the senses (looks good, smells good, tastes good).
2. It must satisfy hunger.
3. It should offer variety.

Of these three areas, variety is by far the most important consideration. If a wide assortment of foods is offered, the senses will be pleased and hunger satisfied. For me, there is nothing more frustrating than to finish a meal and, thirty minutes later, find one of the kids in the kitchen looking for a snack. Satisfying hunger, then, is an important consideration for me.

If someone walks in the front door, sniffs and says, "Lasagne again?" you've probably fallen into a monotonous meal routine. If your meals have become banal and boring, menu planning can give you a change of pace.

Ethel Kennedy, wife of the late Senator Robert Kennedy (and mother of eleven), used a two-week rotating menu plan. In this way she was assured that a meal was never repeated more than once every fourteen days.

Whatever method you use, menu planning will help you remember that you served fried chicken Monday night and maybe Thursday is too soon to have baked chicken on rice. Saving your menu plans from week to week will help you see if something is being repeated too often to provide a good variety. Also, you may be reminded of favorites that haven't been served for a while.

Menu planning is especially valuable to those on restricted

diets. When food selections are limited, it's easy to begin serving the same things over and over again. A written plan will help you stay creative.

It is hard to please everyone at every meal, particularly in a family with children, but menu planning can contribute to a delicate balance by helping you add variety. When a wide assortment of foods is available, everyone can find at least a few things they can enjoy and fill up on.

Goal Number Four: Meals Within Time/Energy Limits

If you were to ask me, "Why do you plan menus?" my immediate answer would be, "Because it saves so much time!" As important and necessary as the other goals are, saving time is my number one reason for menu planning.

When meals are planned with regard to your day's activities you can set realistic time and energy limits. With our four boys, we have frequently been down at the Little League field from 5 P.M. until 9 P.M. On those days I serve tacos or sloppy joes, not beef stroganoff with wild rice. As much as possible, let your calendar or appointment book guide your menu selection so your meal plans fit into available time limits. Ask yourself, "How much time am I willing or able to spend?" There's no reason to plan if the plans cannot be carried out.

Menu planning will save you time because you know in advance what you are fixing and you can eliminate extra or eleventh-hour trips to the store. Since all your supplies and ingredients will be ready to use, your plans will run smoothly, avoiding last-minute changes. How many times have you changed meal plans at the last minute because you didn't have (and couldn't borrow) a missing ingredient? Planning ahead allows you to fix food in advance and dovetail food preparations. You can shave hours off of kitchen time.

So, think before you act. Meal planning will help you reach the goals for a successful meal. But more than that, it will still that harping voice on your mind's periphery asking, "What am I going to fix for dinner?"

A SMORGASBORD OF MENU PLANNING IDEAS

"Be a good cook, " Mother used to say, "and you'll get a man!" What Mother forgot to mention was that you'd also be responsible for planning, preparing and serving about fifty thousand meals throughout the course of your lifetime. (Thanks, Mom.)

Well, times have changed, and we've all come a long way since Mother uttered those famous words. No longer is the kitchen a sanctuary for lovelorn maidens. Men and women alike are beginning to share the responsibility for those fifty thousand meals. If you're the meal manager, you could probably use some menu planning ideas to get you going.

Before you begin, you will need to gather a few supplies: paper, pencil and your favorite recipes. As soon as you're ready, make a list of all the main dishes you serve for dinner. Group these dishes, one type per page—chicken and poultry dishes on one page, ground beef meals on another. The categories I use are beef, ground beef, poultry, fish, pork and miscellaneous. Use the categories that make grouping dishes easiest and most convenient for you. If you're extremely ambitious, you can do the same thing with side dishes such as potatoes, rice and vegetables. If you fix dessert every night, you may want to list desserts, too.

As you list the name of each main course, list all the ingredients needed to make that particular dish. This is not a recipe, just a simple ingredients list. When more than one package or can is needed, indicate it.

SAMPLE MENU SELECTION SHEET:
Chicken

- *Fried Chicken*   Chicken, oil, flour, salt, pepper

- *Chicken and Rice*   Cooked chicken, cream of mushroom soup (2 cans), milk, cooked rice

- *Chicken Broccoli*   Cooked chicken, broccoli (2 pkgs.), cream of chicken soup (2 cans), mayonnaise, lemon juice, cheese, bread crumbs

- *Chicken Noodle*   Chicken, onion, celery, flour, milk, salt, bouillon

- *Chicken Rolls*   Cream cheese (2 small, 1 with chives), margarine, pepper, chicken, chicken broth, cornstarch, crescent rolls, crumbs, chopped walnuts, sage

Right now, you're probably rolling your eyes and thinking, "Sure, when am I going to do all this? I don't even have time to fix dinner!" Don't think of this as a one-shot project. Break it down into little pieces. You can work on the chicken page this afternoon and start fish tomorrow evening. You can do a little during your coffee or lunch break. I know one woman who worked on her sheets while traveling. Break the job down and use snatches of time that would otherwise have been squandered.

Your menu selection sheets may take several pages, depending on your repertoire. But, when you're finished, you'll be in the driver's seat instead of under the rear wheels. These menu selection sheets serve many timesaving purposes. When you're making up menus, you will have all the possibilities right in front of you. There's no need to remember what your family likes because the menu selection sheets have it all recorded. These sheets lift the burden of menu planning. Using them, you can choose one or two items from each page for a week or two of versatile, stimulating meals.

When making your shopping list, refer to your menu selection sheets and you'll have all the ingredient information at your fingertips. No need to check cookbooks or recipe cards to see if you need cream of mushroom or cream of chicken soup, or try to remember if this recipe uses sour cream. And when you're stuck with leftovers, the menu selection sheets can help you choose a good way to use them.

The menu selection sheets serve many other useful purposes. If you like to have surplus food on hand, the menu selection sheets can remind you of the things you'll need to have in reserve. I keep my sheets in my planning notebook. This way if I'm in a store and see a special on round steak, I can easily choose a good way to use it. Also, any extra ingredients that I'll need will not be forgotten. When I find myself waiting at the school or doctor's office, I can plan my menus, because my menu selection sheets are always handy. One of my friends photocopied her menu selection sheets and keeps a copy at work. She can plan menus during coffee and lunch breaks, and should she need to stop at the store on the way home, she's got an accurate and complete ingredients list.

Imagine the fun you'll have running through the grocery ads.

When you notice a great can't-pass-it-up buy, the menu selection sheets will show you all the possibilities for using that bargain. Included with your menu selection sheets (in your planning notebook) you can make notes from January to December listing seasonal fruits and produce. Then, you'll be able to plan effectively for their use.

Save time, save money, and save your family from monotonous meals with the menu selection sheets. Don't leave home without them!

CHOOSE A MENU PLANNING SYSTEM

Once you've completed the menu selection sheets, pick the method that's best suited to your meal planning needs:

1. Get a monthly calendar, the type with large squares. Now, referring to the menu selection sheets, write down in each square what you want to fix for dinner every evening during the month. Be sure to leave a few blanks for leftovers and new recipes to try. If you can't do a whole month, plan a week or two.

I don't especially like to plan menus, so I try to get it over with in one sitting. If, however, you enjoy the activity, you will likely want to do it once a week or so, depending on your time and energy limits. Also, take into consideration how often you want to shop. If you only shop once every two weeks, then menus will have to be planned two weeks in advance.

When it's time to shop, check your menu plans and the ingredients list. Prepare your shopping list by writing down the ingredients you need to prepare your scheduled meals. Just be sure to purchase enough planned ingredients to last from one shopping trip to the next.

Again, having this ingredient list handy is so much easier than going to your cookbook or recipe file to see what you need for every dish.

2. Make up a two-month schedule and rotate all year long. This way, you'll only make menus once in a lifetime. Leave some blank spaces for leftovers and new recipes to try. They can easily be incorporated into your menu selection sheets if they become favorites. With this plan, all you'll have to do is check your ingredients list and make your shopping list.

3. Plan seasonal menus. Try a "plan for all seasons"—a rotat-

ing schedule for fall and spring, schedules for winter meals and summer meals. For some reason, chili, stew and roast turkey taste better on cold winter nights. Grilled meat and fish, fresh fruits and vegetables seem more satisfying in the summer. The "plan for all seasons" can be used to remind you when a supply of a particular food is abundant. Things like strawberries, peaches, sweet corn, and garden fresh tomatoes have a short season. By using a plan, you can take full advantage of the harvest. As with all the other menu planning methods the "plan for all seasons" will allow you to have chicken every Sunday, if that is a family tradition.

4. Rather than assign a certain meal to a specific day, just make a list of ten to fifteen meals. (The number of meals you plan depends on how often you shop.) Within this list, schedule some quick dishes and some that require a little more time. Next, stock up on all the ingredients needed to make these dishes. Then, when you see what the day is going to bring, simply choose one of the meals on your list, picking the one that will best fit the family's circumstances. Your choice may be determined by any of the following factors:

- How much help will be available for dinner preparation?
- How many people will be home to eat the meal?
- How much time will you have to prepare and serve the meal before people scatter?

As you can see, this is a good plan for those who have several conflicting schedules within the family—especially when no one lets you in on the plans until the last minute.

Using any of the meal planning methods, you can incorporate a few other ideas.

Check grocery ads, in-season specials and coupons. Refer to your menu selection sheets and see how you can best use good buys. Referring to the ingredient list, jot down the ingredients necessary to complete your meals.

Ask each family member what he or she would like to have one night during the week (or month). Be sure to round out their ideas to provide adequate nutrition. This menu idea works best when used with one of the four preceding suggestions. All of these systems allow for new recipes, and you can repeat the family favorites as often as you like.

After your menus are planned, go to your deep freeze and bring up all the items you will need for a week. Store these foods in your refrigerator freezer. So many times our dinner plans go awry simply because we don't get the meat defrosted. If your frozen ingredients are handy you'll be more likely to get them thawed and ready. Besides, why make seven trips to the freezer when you need only make one?

If you have a separate food storage area or pantry, bring all the weekly ingredients to your kitchen mixing center and have them handy, too. How many times have you sent someone running to get a can of soup or a box of macaroni? Besides, it's nice to have everything within reach when you're busy fixing dinner.

Remember the time chart for ironing a shirt? The same principle applies here. You can save a lot of time getting ready if you bring everything to the kitchen at once rather than running back and forth every time you're ready to fix a meal.

After you've stocked up on the ingredients for your upcoming meals, it might be helpful to mark those items with a red signal dot or place them all in one special location. This lets the family know that this food is going to be needed, and it's off-limits.

One night we were having beef stroganoff for dinner, and everything was just about ready. All I had to do was add the sour cream to the stroganoff and put it on the table. This particular dish is one of our family's favorites, and everyone was sitting around the table in great anticipation — much like the Bob Cratchit family on Christmas Day. So, I opened the refrigerator to get the sour cream and it was gone.

"Nobody eats plain sour cream." I said. "Where did it go?"

Just then Jeff spoke up, "Oh, I ate it. That stuff is good!" Plain sour cream? One pint?

Needless to say, I'm careful to mark everything or at least let everyone know what things they can't eat.

Keep your menu plans in the kitchen so you can remind yourself first thing in the morning what you have planned. Just knowing what you're going to fix for dinner that night can really lighten your load. You'll also be able to fix what you can after breakfast and thus eliminate some get-ready and clean-up at dinner time.

Remember that getting ready and cleaning up are the two areas where most time is wasted. My best managed days occur when I bake after breakfast and prepare ahead for lunch and dinner. This way, I have eliminated much of the get-ready and clean-up for those remaining meals.

CHAPTER TEN

Accrued Benefits in the Kitchen

Whether you're busy going to and from work or to and from violin lessons, you'll be happy to discover even more ways to provide your family with a nutritious, tasty and quick meal. By using the principle of accrued benefits, you honestly can save time without sacrificing quality.

Accrued benefits really pay off in the kitchen. Maybe you know all about this principle, but how often do you put it into action? Whenever possible, get two for the price of one.

For example, how many times have you doubled a recipe, one to serve and one to freeze? You get the immediate reward (the dinner you serve) and an accumulated reward (the dinner you serve at a later date). That's an accrued benefit. You've had one get-ready, one clean-up and two benefits. That's two for the price of one. Whenever possible, cook with more than one meal in mind. This will not only save precious time but money, as well. Buying larger cuts of meat or buying in quantity is frequently less expensive.

At the risk of sounding redundant, planning ahead is a sure-fire method that always pays big time dividends. Use kitchen time to prepare as much as possible. For example, start tonight's dinner this morning: Prepare a gelatin salad or dessert, chop vegetables for a stir-fry meal, marinate the meat. You can even make extra juice for tomorrow's breakfast, and prepare sandwich fillings for lunch.

All we're doing is combining the clean-up of one job with the get-ready of another. With careful planning, there's no limit to possibilities.

Benefits can grow even larger with careful menu planning.

For example, if you plan chicken chop suey for Monday night, prepare extra rice for Wednesday's filled beef roll. That's two for the price of one.

When planning your menus, try to include as many leftovers as possible. After the principle of accrued benefits becomes a working force in your life, leftovers will be better called "planned-overs"! In the meantime, however, leftovers may be causing a few problems. Many of us put leftovers back into the refrigerator with the best of intentions—"This time I'm going to remember what's in here and use it." Days and days go by, and the leftover collection expands. Pretty soon the refrigerator is so full that we are forced to clean it out. With fear and trembling we open containers wondering what colors and odors await discovery. Most of our good intentions are tossed down the garbage disposal. Sound familiar?

There are a few things you can do to help in your battle against mold and fuzz. First, designate a certain area of your refrigerator where leftovers will be kept. Keep the leftovers in this assigned spot. In our refrigerator the second shelf is for leftovers and other food that needs to be used within a short period of time.

Second, put leftovers in clear containers so it's easier for you to see what's inside, thus reminding you to use the contents.

Third, have a convenient place where you can quickly jot down leftover food, putting the date next to each item. A good place for such a list is inside the cupboard door where most of your food is kept. Hang a small pad and pencil out of sight and you have a quick, efficient place to keep track of your leftovers. Or use a Post-It note, or attach a magnetic clip for notes to the refrigerator door. Whenever you're preparing a meal, check your list to see if any of the leftovers can be incorporated into your meal plans. Cross off anything you use. It will take a few extra seconds to write down an item on this list, but it will eliminate much waste. Over a period of time it will also save you a lot of money.

Start a leftover list and remind the family to use it. Sooner or later, by being reminded of them, you will discover creative ways to use leftovers or to eliminate them. The leftover list also becomes a menu for snackers to choose from. Once you've established the habit of referring to it, you'll see the end of wasted food. It will also cut down on the refrigerator congestion problems.

One good way to use leftovers is to try to include as many as possible in your meal plans. Planning leftovers (prepare extra mixed vegetables for Sunday's fried chicken and use leftovers in Tuesday's beef stew) will give you such a feeling of relief when it's time to prepare a meal, because you'll realize that part of the meal preparations have already been done—and cleaned up! Check your favorite cookbooks and recipes for new ideas using leftovers. In the meantime, here are a few suggestions.

- Vegetables and meats are used well in soups and stews. Leftover roast or ham can be ground and mixed with other ingredients to make a tasty sandwich spread. Leftover beef roast that's been cut into small pieces or shredded can be barbecued or seasoned for use in tacos or burritos. Don't forget the Chinese food possibilities.
- Leftover waffles? Wrap individually and freeze. When they're needed, pop them into the toaster.
- Chicken or turkey can be used in chicken salad or macaroni salad. It can also be barbecued or used in Mexican or Chinese dishes. An array of easy-to-fix poultry casseroles fill the pages of any cookbook. Poultry can also be made into a delicious spread for canapes and other hors d'oeuvres.
- Leftover ham is ideal in chef's salad or in a scalloped potato casserole. There's always ham-potato salad, navy beans and ham, and ham-macaroni salad.
- Pork has many uses in oriental dishes and is especially good heated in barbecue sauce, served in buns.
- Shrimp, tuna, or salmon are used well in salads and sandwich fillings. Creamed tuna or salmon can be the beginning of a flavorful, nutritious meal.
- Beef, lamb or veal can also be served in a variety of casseroles; or, simply heat sliced meat in gravy and serve with potatoes, rice or bread. Don't forget the possibility of homemade meat pies.
- In addition to their use in soups and stews, vegetables can be attractive and nutritious complements to salads and potato-egg dishes.
- Why, you can even make watermelon pickles from the left-

over watermelon rind. Leftover pickle juice can be used to marinate raw vegetables.

With a simple, effective solution to help you keep track of your leftovers and the unlimited possibilities for their use, there's really no reason to waste anything—especially your time!

Try the principle of accrued benefits. At first it may take some deliberate thought, but the time rewards are so satisfying that looking for accrued benefits will soon become second nature!

CHAPTER ELEVEN

Meal Management

I haven't even started dinner and my dish towel is already at half-mast!" Do you ever feel like that? If so, don't despair. It's time for a crash course in meal management. Here we go!

MEAL MANAGEMENT 101

What is management? For some people it's when they manage to get through the day. Actually, efficient management is achieving maximum output with a minimum amount of time and energy. Sounds too good to be true, doesn't it? With good meal management skills, though, it is easily possible.

Here are a few guidelines that will aid you in your pursuit of your meal management degree.

1. Do similar jobs (such as preparing vegetables) consecutively one after the other. Try to work in one area doing tasks simultaneously in the same work center whenever possible. For example, several things can be cooking or baking at the same time.

Remember to work in one area as much as possible. If you followed the basic guidelines for setting up a mixing center in the kitchen, things will be greatly simplified. When you stay in one spot you only need to clean up one spot!

2. Whenever possible, try to complete one task before beginning another. (Prepare all the vegetables; finish setting the table before carving the roast.) Using a time chart (as explained later) will help you establish logical priorities in your meal preparations.

3. Remember that you will probably be interrupted. Make sure your time schedule will allow for the unexpected. If you

could feasibly prepare your planned meal in sixty minutes, allow yourself seventy-five. This will work in extra time for unexpected phone calls, accidental spills and directing family traffic.

4. (This is the most important point to remember.) Clean up as you go—by washing (or rinsing), drying, and putting away the equipment you've used. At least 50 percent of the time we spend cooking is spent waiting. Use this time to clean-up as you go. Whether you're fixing a batch of cookies or preparing a seven-course meal, start by having a sink full of hot, sudsy water. Also have a trash bag nearby. This will speed up those spot clean-ups.

When you open a cake mix, a can of orange juice, a stick of margarine, or whatever, you usually just set the box, can or wrapper on the counter "for now." Pretty soon the mess is growing and your preparation area is taking up more space. When it's time to clean up you have to round up all this trash and toss it away. If you have a garbage bag handy it encourages you to throw things out now, keeping your work area clutter free. You can simply stand your kitchen wastebasket right next to you as you work or hang a plastic grocery bag over a drawer or cupboard handle. Or, take two self-adhesive cup hooks and install them under a cupboard in your working area. That way you can hang up a plastic grocery bag by slipping the handle holes over cup hooks.

Another time saving clean-up tip is to spread a piece of freezer wrap on the counter. You can work right on the paper. It catches all the crumbs, drips and spills, and it's disposable. (Or, use an open brown paper grocery bag or newspaper.)

Imagine yourself sitting down to enjoy a nutritious meal with no visible signs of preparation gracing the countertops or piled in an unsightly mess in the sink. If atmosphere is important in a restaurant, it is equally important at home. Eating is more relaxed and gratifying when you're not surrounded by chaos. It's easier to face after-meal clean-up when the situation is under control. When things don't look too bad, recruits are easier to round up, too.

Return supplies to their places immediately. Remember that it is better to use the same equipment over and over rather than to bring in more equipment. The more you have, the more you have to take care of.

5. Set the table completely during free waiting time. Fill the glasses and put other necessary accessories on the table. Set out serving pieces. The last few minutes before a meal is served are difficult because there are so many details demanding your attention. So, have the table taken care of and out of your way. To simplify setting (and clearing) the table, use a dishpan, tray or wheeled cart so everything can be carried in one trip.

6. Delegate as much as you can without causing kitchen congestion. Too many people in the kitchen is almost as bad as having to do the whole thing alone!

7. When more than one dish requires last-minute attention, prepare first the one that keeps the best. For example, mash the potatoes before you make the gravy.

MANAGING THE BIG MEAL

Once you have mastered the practices listed above, you're ready to tackle a big, important meal. As with any job, using the right tools is important to ensure success. All you need are paper, pencil, recipes and the clock. Whenever I have a large "company's coming" dinner to prepare, I use these tools to make a time chart. It's foolproof—success is guaranteed!

As an example, let's go through the steps necessary to manage a simple Thanksgiving dinner. Consider the following menu: roast turkey with stuffing, mashed potatoes with giblet gravy, sweet potatoes, cranberry sauce, homemade rolls, pumpkin pie. Referring to your menu, make a list of all the little non-food jobs that will be required: Set table, fill glasses, set out dessert dishes and serving pieces and miscellaneous table accessories, bring up extra chairs from the basement, press table linens and napkins, order a centerpiece. The next step is to decide what you can prepare the day before the big meal, such as blueberry salad, cranberry sauce, and turkey broth with giblets for gravy and stuffing.

On the left-hand side of a piece of ruled paper, list the menu. Then, make three vertical columns to the right. Label the columns Prepare; Cook and Ready to Serve; and Total, respectively. In the appropriate column, list how much time it will take to prepare the item for cooking and how much time it takes to cook and/or get the item ready to serve (e.g., assemble and bake the casserole, bake and carve the meat). The two time figures are totaled in the total column.

Menu Item	Prepare	Cook/Ready to Serve	Total Time
Roast Turkey	15 minutes	5 hours	5 hours, 15 minutes
Giblet Stuffing	20 minutes	with turkey	20 minutes
Relish Tray	20 minutes	5 minutes	25 minutes
Mashed Potatoes	10 minutes	35 minutes	45 minutes
Giblet Gravy	5 minutes	10 minutes	15 minutes
Rolls	3.5 hours	30 minutes	4 hours
Sweet Potatoes	5 minutes	30 minutes	35 minutes
Bean Casserole	5 minutes	30 minutes	35 minutes
Pie	Day ahead	5 minutes	5 minutes
Salad	Day ahead	5 minutes	5 minutes
Cranberry Sauce	Day ahead	5 minutes	5 minutes

After your chart is complete, list all menu entries in decreasing order of total time. Here is what the sample menu would look like:

Menu Item	Total Time
Roast Turkey	5 hours, 15 minutes
Rolls	4 hours
Mashed Potatoes	45 minutes
Sweet Potatoes	35 minutes
Bean Casserole	35 minutes
Relish Tray	25 minutes
Giblet Stuffing	20 minutes
Giblet Gravy	15 minutes
Pie	5 minutes
Salad	5 minutes
Cranberry Sauce	5 minutes

For illustration, let's plan to serve dinner at two o'clock. It is possible that this dinner could be prepared in five hours and fifteen minutes—the time required for the turkey. However, to make room for interruptions and to provide a more leisurely atmosphere, let's allow six hours to fix the meal.

Now, referring to the second time chart, work backwards from the serving time and decide when everything needs to be started so dinner will be ready (and cleaned up) at the same time. When gaps or waiting periods appear in your schedule, tuck in small jobs like assembling the relish tray, setting the table, and spot clean-ups. Be sure everything on the menu list and the non-food list is accounted for.

8:00 A.M.	Make stuffing (may also be made the day ahead but do not stuff the turkey until baking time).
8:20 A.M.	Prepare and stuff turkey.
8:30 A.M.	Turkey into oven, vegetable relishes prepared, potatoes peeled — cover with ice water until needed.
8:45 A.M.	Clean-up.
10:00 A.M.	Make rolls, clean-up (may also be made day ahead).
11:45 A.M.	Shape rolls.
12:45 P.M.	Set table, including dessert dishes and serving pieces.
1:00 P.M.	Relish tray assembled, unmold salad, dish cranberry sauce, clean-up.
1:10 P.M.	Potatoes to cook.
1:15 P.M.	Prepare sweet potato casserole and green bean casserole.
1:30 P.M.	Turkey out, casserole and rolls in oven, make gravy.
1:40 P.M.	Potatoes off — mash (warm in oven), clean-up.
1:40 P.M.	Delegate turkey carving and dishing stuffing.
2:00 P.M.	Serve.

Notice there are several clean-up points included in this schedule. Though it sounds tedious, each clean-up requires only a few minutes. Things are so much easier to clean when they are handled immediately. The longer a dish sits around, the longer it takes to clean. After-meal clean-up is greatly simplified when you only have to deal with the dishes and serving pieces. The more pots, pans and mixing bowls you have lying around, the more complicated cleaning up will be.

For those of you who are already efficient meal managers,

these steps are routine and automatic to you. For those of you who struggle, follow these steps and soon you, too, will be able to serve any meal on time and in a clean kitchen!

SHOPPING SHORTCUTS
Before you can have a meal, you have to shop. This is an activity that can benefit from management also. Here's how I do it.

I have a small clipboard with a pad and pencil hanging inside a kitchen cupboard door. The clipboard holds a supply of grocery shopping forms. (These are just 5½″ × 8½″ sheets divided into categories: breads and cereals, canned goods, convenience foods, dairy products and eggs, frozen foods, health and beauty aids, household and miscellaneous, meat, staples, and condiments). Using this form keeps me from chasing back and forth in the store, because the whole list is grouped by category. When you make a linear list you usually write down things when you run out of them. Or you write them in the order they appear in a recipe. So your list could start with olives and tuna and end with pickles. When you get to the bottom of the list you have to go back by the olives to grab a bottle of pickles.

On these forms I write the grocery list I have compiled from my menu selection sheets. Also, when I run out of a certain item, I simply open my cupboard door, grab the pencil and jot it down. These forms also make lists easy for other family members to use and contribute to. This way I always have a grocery list on hand, and I won't forget a needed item. On the back of the grocery shopping form I jot down the dinner meals I've planned for the next week or so.

When I'm ready to go shopping, I put the grocery list right into my planning notebook. At the store, the notebook stands in the child's seat, or a child can hold it. The list is easily visible, and I can cross out items as I take them from the shelves. Instead of using the planning notebook, you can just grab the clipboard and take it to the store. In addition to your shopping list, the clipboard can hold coupons you're going to use, bottle deposit receipts or trading stamps.

Make the most of the time you spend shopping. We've already discussed how meal planning can eliminate unnecessary and frequent trips to the store, but here are a few other techniques that will help conserve time.

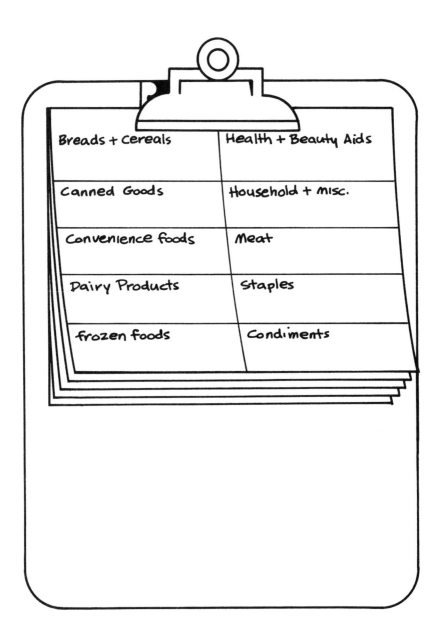

Breads + Cereals	Health + Beauty Aids
Canned Goods	Household + misc.
Convenience foods	Meat
Dairy Products	Staples
frozen foods	Condiments

Categorized shopping lists eliminate the need for emergency trips to the store

1. Limit shopping trips, as much as possible, by keeping reserve supplies on hand. If you have plenty of storage space and keep it stocked, you will be able to reduce the number of shopping excursions. This need not be expensive. Coupons, refunds, and special case lot sales can reduce your costs considerably.

2. Shopping from an organized list can speed you through supermarket aisles. Print up a form for your grocery list. Some categories to include might be dairy, canned goods, produce, meat, frozen foods, bakery, spices and condiments, household (cleaners, gadgets, detergents) health and beauty aids, pet supplies, and miscellaneous non-food. When you have your form completed, photocopy several to keep on hand. As you run out of a needed item, jot it down on the printed form placing it in its proper category. When you're shopping you will have everything grouped and will eliminate time spent backtracking.

Some experts suggest making a list organized according to the way your favorite market is arranged. This format is not as versatile because it functions well only in that particular store. Also, when stocks of merchandise are rearranged, your printed list becomes obsolete.

3. Shop at a time of day and on a day of the week when congestion is at a minimum. Call the store manager and ask when the best time is. Also check to see if the advertised specials will still be available at that time. Ask if there will be adequate stock to choose from and about the availability and freshness of produce and bakery products. There's no point shopping during low traffic hours if you can't complete your entire list.

4. Get into the habit of replacing things before the supply is exhausted. As soon as you notice something is running low, add it to your list.

I've even made a list of everything I never want to run out of again. Things like milk, bread, catsup, popcorn, Kleenex and dishwasher detergent are on that list. I try to keep at least two of each of these high-priority items on hand. As soon as the one in storage is put into use, I put it on the shopping list and replace it. That way, I never have to run out of those things again.

5. Whenever possible, pack your own groceries. That way, things that belong in certain areas of your house can be grouped

together and will take much less time to put away.

With rising prices and tight time schedules, I've come to regard shopping as a necessary evil. Even though it may never be a heavenly experience, I try to make it less painful by sacrificing as little of my time as possible.

PART THREE

OTHER ROOMS,
OTHER PEOPLE

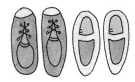

CHAPTER TWELVE

Turning Toyland Into Joyland

When our first baby was born, I couldn't believe how much room that little guy took up. Blankets, quilts, diapers, high chair and changing table took an extensive toll on our available space. What I didn't realize was that it would get worse . . . fast! A quilt can be folded neatly and placed on a closet shelf, but what do you do with the dried corncobs your little boy likes to push around with his bulldozer?

I know a woman who hadn't seen one of her daughter's dresses for weeks. One day it was unearthed from under three feet of debris on the closet floor. Believe me, I can understand. I've learned from experience that three thousand baseball cards can hide almost anything. As I write this I think three thousand baseball cards wouldn't be so bad. We're now somewhere in the neighborhood of sixty thousand cards.

Then, there's the car. When we travel with the children, I usually arrive at our destination sitting cross-legged, Indian fashion, in the front seat. The reason for the Lotus position is that the car floor is heaped so high with trash, shoes, toys, crayons and half-eaten hamburgers there is no room for my feet.

As you can see, toys and assorted wreckage have caused more home management problems than unemployment. If you are wringing your hands wondering what to do, the best way to spell relief is *organize*.

But where do you start? The hard part about organizing your kids' stuff is that your offspring are usually unorganizing faster than you can organize. But don't fret. Let's get started in the toy department and put an end to some of this disorganization.

Do you put all your kids' toys into a toy box, then wonder why your children never play with their toys? Or do you spend hours making toy bags and feel frustrated when your kids dump everything out to find what they want?

STORAGE OPTIONS FOR TOYS

As soon as our number-one child got old enough to play and began to accumulate a collection of toys, we rushed right out and got him a toy box. Every child had to have a toy box, I thought. But things were always a mess in that toy box, and I couldn't stand it. I tried to organize it, putting cars and trucks here, building blocks there, but to no avail. Every evening I was on my knees in front of the toy box — not praying for help (which I obviously needed), but rearranging and putting things back in place. It drove me nuts!

Next, I tried another storage option — hanging. Thinking there had to be a workable solution to this confusion, I sat right down and sewed up a bunch of drawstring toy bags. I sorted and categorized each group of toys (again) into separate bags and hung them up in the toy closet. Feeling much like Betsy Ross must have felt after finishing the flag, I stood back to admire my toy bag creations.

Then came the true test — children. The toy bags were hard for them to handle, and in order to choose a specific toy, they had to dump everything on the floor. (I did find a way to make this idea work — read on.)

Next, I tried shelving. Here's where I found the storage alternative that worked best for us.

I got an old bookshelf and organized toys on the shelves. Again, dishpans came to the rescue. I had a dishpan for each of the following: Legos, blocks, small vehicles, Barbie dolls, Barbie accessories, cowboy gear. Smaller things were contained in rectangular planters (about the size of half a dishpan) made out of heavy plastic. These were well-suited for things like Fisher-Price people and furniture, small plastic cowboys and Indians, animals and spacemen.

Plastic ice cream pails work well, too. They can also be hung from hooks, and they have lids that help to stop some dumping. However, as with any round container, they waste space. So, if you're short on space, avoid anything round. One added feature of the ice cream pails, though — they're free!

Each toy container was labeled with a permanent black marker so we'd know what belonged where. Hand-drawn pictures or pictures cut from magazines can be used to identify the contents of the container for youngsters who can't read. They should also know where things belong.

I used two rectangular laundry baskets for storage as well. One was used to hold large vehicles, the other was used for large adventure-set things that were always used together.

Now, every little thing has a place. When we see something out of place, we can quickly put it into its proper container. Although the kids still occasionally dump out the contents of a container, they can usually choose just the toy they want.

Remember, you don't need an actual bookcase or built-in shelves for toys. Shelves can be built with particle board and stacked bricks, cement blocks, or large cans of food. Inexpensive snap-together metal shelves or study cardboard shelves can be purchased at any discount store. Lightweight shelves can be anchored to a wall to keep children from toppling them. They come in many different sizes and are a storage bargain. You don't need fancy, expensive equipment to get organized. Use your imagination and try to make do with the space and materials available to you. If we always made the most of our resources, we would all be much happier.

My in-depth research (through trial and error) led me to discover the best toy storage alternative for me. And I learned something along the way. Each of the storage alternatives for toys had different advantages. To help you choose what will work best for you (without so much trial and error) let's consider the pluses and minuses of each option.

Toy Box Terrors

The most obvious storage method is, of course, the toy box. The toy box has a few marked advantages. First of all, it can be decorative, adding to the overall look of a room. It also keeps the toys hidden from view, which makes the room more pleasing to the eye. Toy boxes usually require only a small amount of floor space, which may be a prime consideration for those living in cramped quarters. Some toy boxes, depending on the shape, provide a perfect storage area for bats, balls and otherwise cumbersome equipment, or even large toys.

However, the toy box usually becomes a hollow space in which to dump any given number of things. In order to make a toy box system truly functional, the toys need to be grouped and divided so the children can find and use what they want. Keeping the system going requires daily maintenance.

Sometimes a standard toy box is not large enough to accommodate all the toys, so an additional storage method has to be used. (Drawers, by the way, have the same advantages and disadvantages as toy boxes.)

Toy Bags

Another common storage option is the toy bag. These are bags with drawstring openings made from any kind of fabric. The bags can be made from a fabric that coordinates with the room decoration. To overcome the problem of the child who dumps the entire bag to see what's inside, try these ideas. With words or pictures, label the bags so the children will know what is contained inside. A clear plastic "window" can also be sewn on the bag, so the child can get a better view.

The bags are usually kept hanging on an available wall or other vertical space. Because they are stored in a hanging position, the bags make use of what would otherwise be wasted space. Saving space, then, would be a positive benefit from toy bags. Another benefit is that they cannot be easily dumped by toddlers.

But toy bags also have several disadvantages. My main objection is that they are hard to handle. When a bag contains small vehicles, for example, it's hard for a child to get the red Jeep (or other favorite car) without pouring the contents of the bag on the floor. Toy bags are better suited for complete toy sets that are always used together, not separately.

Also, it is difficult for a child to put toys back into a toy bag. He has to hold the bag with one hand while the other little hand drops a few things at a time into the bag's opening. Once the bags are hanging it is sometimes awkward to put a stray, forgotten piece back in.

So, toy bags can be decorative, they can save space, and they can be kept out of the reach of young children. However, they are hard to handle and will require extra time when toys are put away.

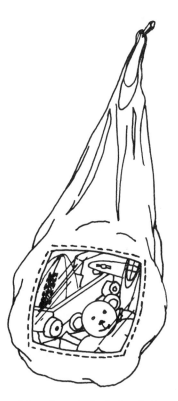

A hanging toy bag with a clear vinyl window helps youngsters see the contents

Storing Toys on Shelves

The last storage option is shelving. Using this method the toys are categorized and put into dishpans, ice cube bins, cardboard boxes, laundry baskets—preferably anything square or rectangular in shape. Plastic ice cream pails, though round, are free, and have lids that can discourage those little toddlers. The pails can also be hung up. That way, kids get one-motion storage by easily selecting just what they want without dropping things out on the floor. It is extremely easy to sort and return toys to their respective cartons or pails, again using one motion.

When our children were young, I put large, lightweight things on the bottom shelves (i.e., Fisher-Price farm, garage, airport) and the individual bins containing vehicles, blocks and action figures were placed on higher shelves. This served two purposes. (1) It kept the children from constantly dumping everything. (2) When the kids wanted something from a higher shelf they had to ask for it. That way I could say, "Sure, I'll get your dishes but first pick up your car wash set."

Open shelves of toys are not decorative and give the appearance of clutter, so they are best kept in a closet or behind a screen or blind.

Learn from my mistakes. Weigh the advantages and disadvantages of each toy storage method and choose the right one for you.

More Toy Storage Ideas

After buying the toy box, the next thing we purchased for our firstborn was a small bookcase. We bought him scores of books (of course he had to be the brightest child on the block) and we needed someplace to keep them. With the books on a bookshelf, all the child could see were these nondescript, thin spines. There they were—fifty books all looking pretty much the same. The only way he could pick out a book was to deposit them all over the floor.

Frustrated again, I struck gold. I bought a heavy plastic kitty litter pan (a shallow, corrugated box would also work) and put it on the closet floor. There I stood the books in the pan with the covers facing forward. The pan is wide enough for two rows of small books side by side. A child can flip through the books (like file folders) without having to disturb them. Making a selection is easy, and the bright, illustrated book covers act as an invitation to read. (And the best news of all is that kitty-litter pans now come in decorator colors!)

You may need more than one book box, and maybe you'd like to keep your box of books on a shelf. I chose the floor because there was no place else for our child's books to go, and even a small child could easily use the book collection. Many times over the years, I've seen one of our children curled up in a corner by the floor library looking at a book.

If you decide to store the kitty litter pan on a shelf, put it on the bottom shelf. That will discourage dumping. The kitty litter pan will also save you some space. The pan (approximately 12″ × 8″) will store about 114 standard Golden Books in 18 inches of bookshelf space. Stored in the regular fashion, 114 books would use nearly 24 inches.

This same idea can be used for any compact discs or tapes the kids may have. The kitty pan (as well as some dishpans) will confine them, and standing them up makes titles easy to read and select.

Ice cube bins are also durable containers that can be used to organize a number of things. For your child's coloring book collection, stand the coloring books in a dishpan, and in front of the coloring books put an ice cube bin to hold crayons, scissors, markers, etc. Or, make a coloring book caddy out of a clean-up caddy. The coloring books stand up in the back and markers and crayons, etc. are stored in the two cubby hole containers in the front section of the clean-up caddy. When your child wants to color, he can grab the dishpan or caddy and have everything he needs in a portable container. Ice cube bins are also good receptacles for book and record sets. Or you can use the bins as toy organizers on your toy shelf.

Now, with things organized, our kids spend more time playing with their *toys*, instead of the boxes they came in!

WHERE SHOULD THE TOYS BE KEPT?

The most important and basic organizing principle regarding toys is grouping—having one central location for all of the toys. Ideally, this central location should not be in a child's bedroom (particularly if there is more than one child in the family).

Let's say Jim has his toys stored in his room and Mary has hers stored in her room. Here's what usually happens. When Jim's room is totaled, everyone simply packs up and moves to Mary's room. Shortly, Mary's room is in as bad a shape as Jim's. The toys are scrambled together and mixed up. When cleaning time inevitably rolls around you have to sort the toys by ownership before they can be returned to their rightful places.

It's so much faster and easier to put all the blocks in one bin and all the crayons in another. If you expect other people to help you keep things in order, eliminate as many decisions and movements as you can. In other words, make your system simple. Which sounds easier—running from room to room distributing a few toys here and a few toys there or gathering all the toys and depositing them in one central area?

Another reason for not keeping toys in a bedroom is that toys add to the cluttered look of a room. It is especially important to a child that his or her room have a neat appearance. When things always look jumbled, the child learns to tolerate a mess. There's no opportunity to discover how pleasant order feels. In a neat-looking room, when a bed is left unmade or clothing is thrown on the floor, it is more obvious that these things are out of place. In a room that looks slightly chaotic to begin with a few more things strewn here and there will not make much difference.

So whenever possible, choose one central location for all the toys. This could be a closet, an available wall or an entire room. Remember, we've been talking in terms of the ideal. In reality the design or size of a home sometimes makes it impossible to store toys anywhere but the bedrooms. In that case, choose a storage alternative or a combination of storage alternatives that will allow you easy maintenance and a look of order.

One home we lived in posed a problem for toy storage. The basement was cold and unfinished so it wasn't well-suited as a toy depot and I didn't want to keep the toys in the kids' small bedroom. The solution that worked best was this: We stored all the toys in the basement, and we let the children bring the toys upstairs to play with. As toys accumulated here and there throughout the day, we put them in a large, plastic wastebasket that was placed in one of the kids' bedroom closets. Before bed each night, we took the filled basket downstairs and quickly re-placed the toys.

Try to make the most out of what you have to work with. As long as you're using an easy maintenance system that gives you the look of order, you're on the right track.

SOLVING THE PUZZLE

When our first child was about two, his dad bought him three Popeye puzzles. The puzzles had about forty pieces each, so I put them up until I thought Jimmy was old enough to do them. As he approached age three, Jim started to ask me for those puzzles. Day after day I told him that the puzzles were too hard. Day after day he persisted. Finally, I got the puzzles down just to prove to him I was right. Needless to say, he sat down and quickly put all three puzzles together.

Since that day, our kids have had a certain fascination for puzzles. I could handle the inlaid puzzles all right. (These puzzles are the kind that come in a frame tray.) They stacked nicely, and since I coded each piece, they were never much of a problem, as long as I kept the stack high enough. I must admit that a few times we've had to pick up and put together twenty-five puzzles at the same time. If only I hadn't trusted a two-year old not to get into them!

I code the inlaid puzzles for storage as follows: Each puzzle piece is given a letter and the tray where the pieces fit is given the same letter. That way we always know what piece goes with what puzzle. They stack up neatly on a shelf. But have you ever seen those giant puzzles? They present quite a different storage problem. What I do with ours is code the puzzle and put all the pieces in a small (but wonderful) Ziploc food storage bag. On the bag I mark on masking tape or a self-adhesive label the letter of the puzzle. Then I stand the large puzzle trays in a closet corner. You can either store the bags separately, or clamp them to the puzzle tray.

As I said earlier, I could handle the inlaid puzzles. But as our children's skills increased, the puzzles got more complicated. They graduated to jigsaw puzzles (the kind without the tray). No problem, I thought. Those dandy puzzle boxes will be a snap to store. (Yes, I have the word *stupid* written on my forehead.) Little did I realize that those "dandy puzzle boxes" last long enough for you to do the puzzle about twice. With puzzle boxes and my nerves falling apart at the same rate, I knew I would either have to totally ban puzzles or hope for the manufacturer to recall them. I began to get the old toy box terrors again.

Well, American manufacturing came to my rescue again with those incredible Ziploc food storage bags. I took all the puzzle boxes and cut out the small sample pictures from the sides of the boxes. Then I gave each puzzle a number and numbered all the puzzle pieces. When a jigsaw puzzle is first put together you can pick it up in one piece, turn it over and write the numbers on the back of each piece. This will be a job if you already have several puzzles. Just do each puzzle after it's been put together. Gradually, your whole collection will be coded. By the way, it takes less than five minutes to code a one-thousand-piece puzzle.

If your puzzle collection is not too large, color coding is an easy alternative. Just run a colored marker over the backs of all the pieces.

I put each jigsaw puzzle in a separate Ziploc bag. Most of our puzzles (seventy or so) fit into the one-quart size. This size bag holds five hundred pieces, but not one thousand. As I described previously, I mark the puzzle number on masking tape or a self-adhesive label, and stick it on the bag. Then I stand the bags up in numerical order in a cardboard tray.

I use small pictures of each puzzle to make a catalog that works like a sewing pattern catalog. I glue the pictures on paper and write the puzzle number beneath them. (If a small picture isn't printed on the side of the box, I just use the large, front panel.) The catalog pages are then put in a ring binder. The children look through the catalog and decide which puzzle they want. They see what number it is and go to the puzzle bag with the same number. When I find a puzzle piece on the floor, I pick it up, read the number on it, and pop it into the proper bag.

HELP FOR THE LEGO MANIAC

I frequently field a lot of questions about how to store Legos. Seems like everyone has his favorite storage method. Some people store them by color. They have separate dishpans (or whatever) for red, white, yellow, green, and accessory pieces. Other folks save the original boxes and store the various sets inside. I also know of people who store their collections in five-gallon plastic containers with lids. Do you have a big, empty drawer somewhere? That's an option. You could also use a drawstring bag.

GAMES PEOPLE PLAY

You may not be aware that game boxes are made by the same people who make puzzle boxes. Thus, they are equally durable. If you have even one game, chances are you have used tape, staples, rubber bands and cement to hold the box together. Games are expensive, and we need to protect our investment, right?

Games have caused me more grief than anything over the years. When I straighten the game closet, I put the largest box on the bottom and stack all the boxes in a neat pile with the smallest box on top. This pyramid storage system works very well as long as no one ever uses a game. But when someone wants Scrabble, they pull it out from the bottom of the stack. Naturally, when it's put away it goes right on top. The result? An upside-down pyramid that soon descends upon the next unsuspecting game player.

Once again I was at the mercy of flimsy cardboard boxes. My husband said sweetly, "You just have to be smarter than the box." Charming man. My frustration led me to a metal parts cabinet, the kind with the plastic drawers. Before I went shopping for this cabinet, however, I analyzed just how much space each game would need. Sorry doesn't have too many accessories, Monopoly and Life have a lot. That gave me an idea of the size of drawers we would require. I also counted how many drawers I would need to have. This number included a few extras, though, to allow for new games that would be added to our collection.

I went to a discount store and found just what I needed. There

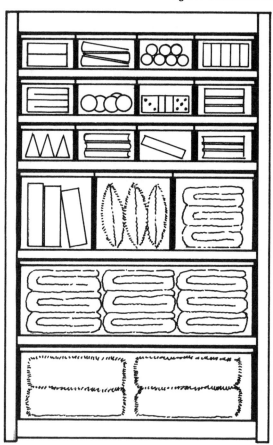

A metal parts cabinet is a great system for storing games

are chests with large drawers, medium-sized drawers and small drawers. There are chests that have drawers of different sizes and chests with drawers all of the same size. (If you decide on this type of chest, be sure all the drawers aren't the small size.) I chose the type I wanted, brought it home, and put all the game pieces in the drawers. Each drawer is labeled, and some drawers are big enough to hold more than one game. The drawers come with drawer dividers so you can alter the size of the storage spaces within each individual drawer.

You will, of course, run into games that can't be adapted to this idea, like Mr. Mouth, Battleship and Black Tower. It is convenient, though, to keep the Mr. Mouth chips and the Battleship pegs in the drawers. It's so much easier to put stray pieces back into the cabinet than it is to wrestle with the boxes. Even though you will have to keep some of the game cartons, you will save a lot of space by using this simple game storage method.

Warning: When you're using drawer storage, small children can dump the contents of twenty-five games all at once. So, take care. When our children were very young I kept the game cabinet on a high shelf with the drawers facing the wall (so it wouldn't look even remotely interesting). When they wanted a game they had to have someone get it for them. We just slide out the drawer, grab the game board, and we're ready to play.

I labeled the game boards with self-adhesive labels and stood them up between the chest and the wall. We just flip through them like file folders and take the one we're looking for. Since all the game boards look alike when they're closed, labeling keeps us from having to open each board to see which one it is.

I put all the game directions in a loose-leaf notebook in alphabetical order. Some game directions are printed on the box lid, thus necessitating photocopying. (And yes, I felt like a fool going into the copy center with a stack of mutilated game box lids under my arm.) A pocket inside the front cover of the same notebook holds any game spinners, score pads and instruction booklets.

Now when I find a Monopoly house, it easily finds its way home. During a game, if a question about the game rules arises, we simply turn to the direction book. What used to take two shelves now fits nicely on a half shelf. See, we could all live in smaller houses if we got organized. What a great way to fight inflation.

CHAPTER THIRTEEN

Reflections on Collections

T he collected mementos of my entire young life would probably fill a dress box. So, I never gave much thought to how I'd store my children's school papers and childhood keepsakes. I'd simply put all their things into a dress box in chronological order. Then in eighteen years, I'd just hand my child his whole life.

Life has taught me many humbling lessons. What our oldest child brought home the first day of kindergarten could easily have filled a dress box. How many blows can one person endure?

Well, I muddled through this sea of papers and watched the rising tide as each of our children went to school. I was getting used to the mess when I realized there was far more than papers collecting. Did you know that kids save used pieces of sandpaper, broken golf tees, and leather covers from old baseballs? What a revelation that was for me.

A FIVE-STEP SYSTEM

I found five simple things that take care of all this debris: in/out baskets, holding file, scrapbook, treasure box, and a junk container. Here's how it works.

In and Out Baskets

Each one of our kids has a plastic vegetable bin that we call their in and out baskets. When the kids come home from school, they toss their books and school papers into their bins. If they've received mail or magazines during the day, I put it into their bins. If I have to sign permission slips, report cards, send money or egg cartons to school, that stuff is put into their bins—not on the kitchen table to remind me to give it to them.

Of course, I have to clean these bins out occasionally because old spelling tests and math worksheets sift to the bottom. Most things I just check and throw out. I am on the lookout, though, for treasures. These are things that have historical value—things we want to keep forever (cards from Grandma, report cards, creative stories, photographs).

I try to keep a cross section of things so we can always remember what that period of the child's life was really like. I want a true picture showing likes and dislikes, struggles and strengths. For example, I saved a social studies test that showed a booming score of 14 percent. What was a devasting blow to me will be a riot to a grown adult when he reads that Kansas City is a state, and a ghetto is a network of underground subway systems! I saved a marriage proposal written on the back of a second grade Valentine's card. I have saved Indiana Jones bubblegum cards and pictures of Michael Jackson, Van Halen, Mr. T., and The New Kids On The Block. Now, if only I had a picture of Wal-Mart (our home away from home), my collection would be complete.

One of our kids (better known as the note-writing phantom) left messages all over the house so we'd know where he was. It wasn't uncommon to step out of the shower and see a note taped to the glass door. "Steven is at Benjie's hose." (He didn't know how to spell house.) When waking from a catnap, we were likely to find notes taped to our arms, legs or stomachs: "Steven is at Troy's." So, we've saved a few of these notes to remind us of this stage in his life.

If you're going to save these valued keepsakes, spend the few extra seconds it takes to label them. If nothing else, indicate the child's name and the date. We have a drawing of that famous story, "Noah's Ark, the Dove and the Alligator." If I hadn't labeled that alligator, we'd still be wondering what the green thing was swimming around the Ark.

Another time I was going through one of the bins and found a wadded-up, torn piece of paper. I smoothed it out, wondering why I had ever saved such an obvious piece of junk. Then I saw a note I had written: "This was the speech Brian gave when he ran for mayor of the third grade." How grateful I was that I had spent five or ten seconds to write that sentence. I had made a treasure out of something that otherwise would have been trash.

Here are some storage options for the in and out baskets. I

use narrow, plastic vegetable bins. They're narrow and don't take up a lot of space. I keep them on a low cupboard shelf in the kitchen. (You can't see them; they're behind a cupboard door.) I keep them in the kitchen because in our house, that's where everything is always dumped. The kitchen seems to be the most convenient repository.

Other containers to use include dishpans, a portion of a bookshelf, a deep drawer. A book bag or backpack could be hung up to collect children's treasures. A cardboard shoe file is another inexpensive, durable option. You can find these in the closet department at discount stores. They're approximately 25 inches wide, 13 inches high and 13 inches deep and are divided into nine cubby holes. Your shoe file fits on a closet shelf or on the floor. Unless you have nine children, you won't need to use all nine of the cubby holes. You could use one cubby hole for "in" and another one for "out." Extra cubby holes could be used for paper, envelopes, a dictionary or phone books. If you put shoe boxes without the lids into the cubby holes, you'll have drawers for coupons, pens, pencils, and other school supplies or what have you.

The Holding File

OK. That takes care of the in/out baskets. Let's move on to the holding file. I've cleaned out the in/out baskets, culling unwanted items. That leaves me with a collection of keepsakes. What then? I simply put them in the holding file. This is just a place where they're kept safe, sound, and out of the way until we have a chance to put them into scrapbooks.

The holding file can be just about anything: a box filled with file folders (one for each person); stacking letter trays (like office workers use); a cardboard shoe file; dishpans—whatever. It is helpful, though, to have a separate container for each person. Stored in this way the things are safe and fairly chronological. And if someone wants to peruse his waiting collection or work on his scrapbook, he can just grab his things without having to sift through the whole pile.

At least once a year the holding file should be emptied out and its contents put in scrapbooks.

Storing these collections needn't be time-consuming. Most of us dread tedious hours spent mounting pictures, filling in baby books and fussing with scrapbooks. There are easier ways that can be very effective. For example, every year put each person's collection into a separate manila envelope. Label the envelope with the person's name and the year. Keep the envelopes filed in chronological order, and you'll have a life story told with photographs, artwork, school work and other reminders. You could also put the year and person's picture on the front of the envelope, then keep the envelopes in a looseleaf ring binder.

The Scrapbook

Each one of our kids has a scrapbook and over the years each book has become a cherished possession. We have a very simple system. We use two-inch looseleaf binders and mount everything on margin reinforced looseleaf paper. Special keepsakes are stored with plastic sheet protectors. We use tabbed dividers to denote and separate each year. For us, one notebook holds about ten years. (You may have more photos and keepsakes, so your notebook will hold fewer years.)

There are some items, especially artwork, that presents problems. Sometimes we have to trim a little off the margin, or once in a while the picture is so large that we fold it. Most of the school artwork is displayed in the house for a few weeks, then (except for rare exceptions) it is thrown out. Sometimes it takes the sting away if you'll take a picture of the child holding the piece before you throw it away. That way you keep the memory and not the masterpiece. Photos are an especially helpful way to save some of the three-dimensional things children have to do for school: diaramas, relief maps, Popsicle stick colonies, animals, etc. Our daughter's class had to make dragons out of anything: papier mâché, clay, sugar cubes, fabric—anything—as long as it stood up. In other words, the dragon couldn't be flat. She made hers out of Legos. This was an ideal project to photograph and save.

Our oldest child has a scrapbook to die for. Every year I worked on Jim's life story and included it in his scrapbook. But as the years went by and more kids came along, I got busier and busier. For years, the rest of our kids had produce boxes in the basement filled with stuff. To simplify things a little, I typed up a questionnaire and had the kids fill one out every year. These questionnaires have given us revealing (though not time-consuming) thumbnail sketches of their lives.

1. If you could trade places with someone else, who would it be?
2. If you could go anywhere on vacation, where would you like to go?
3. What famous person do you admire most? Why?
4. Who are your favorite movie stars, singers and sports figures?
5. What is your favorite sport, favorite movie and favorite song?
6. What do you remember about your last school year?
7. What would you like to change about yourself?
8. What would you like to change about the world?
9. What do you like to do in your spare time?
10. If you had a million dollars, how would you spend it?

Not only are these questions stimulating and fun for the children to answer, they are also effective and revealing for adults. As for the kids, I am always surprised how their answers change from year to year.

Photographs

I don't think I've ever given a seminar (and I've presented over a thousand) where someone didn't ask me what to do with photographs. First, label them. Today you remember the occasion and the names of everyone in the picture. Left unmarked, will that picture mean anything to you twenty years from now?

When the boys were very small I didn't bother to label pictures. I thought surely I would remember all the details about my own kids! I was sadly mistaken. Sometimes when I look at those old photos, the only way I can tell which boy is in the picture is to look at the carpet he's sitting on. (We moved a lot and each boy was a baby in a different house.)

If you're terribly ambitious or if you have a large photograph collection, you might want to start a photo-negative file. I have received many calls and letters from people asking what to do with photo negatives. I didn't have the faintest idea, so I consulted some experts.

Our local state historical society recommended the following catalog system: Number each one of your pictures. Write the number on the back of the picture and write it underneath the

---

FIGHTING FEAR AND SENTIMENT

In this arena, collections, you'll need to fight fear and sentiment head on. Employ the basic organizing principles with
abandon:

1. Think before you act.
2. Discard and sort.
3. Group.
4. Be motion-minded.
5. Practice preventive maintenance.
6. Use your accrued benefits.

As you sort, ask yourself:

1. Do I really need this?
2. Do I need so many?
3. Will I care for this person any less if I give this away?

---

picture if it's mounted permanently in an album or book. Then,
number each negative to correspond with its printed picture.
For example, the picture of Johnny at Sea World would be number one. The negative of the same picture would also be number
one.

Number each negative in the margin with India ink. Use a
straight-steel dip pen or technical drawing pen, or a fountain
pen with a fine point, since there's not much room in the margin
to write on. (Permanent felt-tip marker will work but it is not as
permanent as India ink.)

The negatives can be stored in a number of ways. Several
numbered negative strips can be placed in an envelope. Number
the envelope to correspond with the numbers on the negative
(e.g., this envelope holds negatives numbered one through forty-
eight). Negative holders called glassine or plastic sleeves are
available commercially. They come in a variety of sizes and can
be filed in negative file boxes (also available commercially) or
looseleaf notebooks.

Some people have told me that they just throw away their
negatives. If they want copies of a certain picture, they give the
picture to the photo store, and they make copies from that. Pur-
ists, I suppose, would scoff—but it works for me!

The historical society cautions that mounting papers, glues

and pens should all be acid-free to keep the pictures from breaking down. They say, too, that it's wise to take occasional black-and-white pictures, because over time the color photos will fade.

There are many styles and types of photo albums on the market that hold all sizes of photographs. Check a few camera shops, and see what organizers are available.

If you have a backlog of photo envelopes stuffed with pictures, all you need to do is to start sorting. Most of us procrastinate about doing this because it seems so overwhelming, and we don't have a large block of time available to work on it. Here's how to do it painlessly. First collect all the loose photographs you can find. Go through drawers, boxes, cupboards, attics — everywhere you've stashed bits of your collection. (If things are really scattered, just gather from one room a day or whatever your time will allow.) Once you have all the pictures corralled, then you're ready to sort. Decide, first, how you are going to sort these pictures. Are you going to give some pictures to specific people? Are you going to keep them all, and put them in chronological order? Decide what categories you need, and label several file folders accordingly. (When I did this, I got a dishpan and stood up six file folders inside — one for each child and one for my husband and me).

Next, begin sorting. Pick a photo out of the box and put it into the proper file folder. You can work on this for fifteen minutes or two hours — whatever time you've allotted. When you're tired or have to stop, put your box of photos and file folders out of the way in a corner. There's no mess and you can work on the sorting process during any small snatch of time — while watching TV, talking on the phone, or waiting for the spin cycle to finish. You could even stick the project in the car, and work on it while you're waiting for soccer practice to end or on the way to work (if you're a passenger). Once you've finished this primary sorting job, you may have to sort each file individually by year. When that's done, then you're ready to mount the pictures into scrapbooks.

When you're feeling energetic, organizing negatives, slides and photos ought to keep you out of mischief for a while!

Treasure Box (aka Junk Container)
So, we have things in scrapbooks, but that still leaves things like the wooden train engine Grandma gave our son Jim for his

first Christmas, the ceramic apple our daughter Schuy made for Mother's Day, the mosaic paperweight, and the ubiquitous plaster handprints. Of course, you'll want to display and use some of these things. But there comes a time when they'll have to be tucked away to make room for some new things. That's where the treasure boxes come in. You just need some kind of a covered container — an under-the-bed box, cardboard file box, produce box, plastic storage box, a trunk, cedar chest or footlocker. Depending on how many things you have, you might want one box for each person. We've pretty much contained our collection in an antique trunk.

Don't forget to label these things. Just write a brief explanation on a piece of masking tape and stick it to the object. If you're afraid the adhesive on the tape will damage some items, just write a descriptive, identifying note on a piece of paper or note card. Then, pack the item and description together.

Now, the school papers, mementos and photos are under control, but there's still the matter of empty Chapstick cases, Pez dispensers, Garfield bike reflectors, jelly bracelets, bouncy balls and Happy Meal periscopes. Personally, I can't stand to see all this stuff, and I refuse to clean around it. However, I don't feel that I should inflict my wishes on my children by making them throw everything away. After all, I don't want to mess with their psyches. Seems I read somewhere about a guy who blamed his trouble with the law on his mother. She'd never let him keep things that were important to him. I think he ended up being some kind of a disgruntled employee or something.

I don't have the ultimate solution, but I have a few ideas. Children need to have a place for their things. Without a well-confined place for their "treasures," you will have piles of papers and baseball cards on their dressers, and stacks of refuse on the floor.

A kitty litter pan or dishpan can be used for storage if the problem isn't too severe. Large, covered, under-the-bed boxes could be an answer, too. Our boys each used a drawer in a nightstand. One of their weekly jobs was to straighten their "junk" drawers.

Whatever type of container you give them for this junk, it'll be more effective if it doesn't have a lid. Children are toss-ers. They are not put-ers, and lids require putting. Also, when the containers get full they have to throw some stuff out to make room for some new plunder. Teach them how to throw things away when they're young. That way they won't grow up to be the type of people who take junk to the dump and come home with more than they took. (I heard a lady at the checkout of a secondhand store tell the clerk, "I drop it off at the back door and take it out the front door.")

Here's another optional organizer: a large magazine file box. If your children are like ours, they likely have a hoard of "important" papers. (Over the years I've seen things like unmailed letters to Pete Rose, Barbie magazines, a Walter Payton autograph, a Wheaties box with Michael Jordan on the front, the wedding plans our fifth-grade daughter wrote up for her friend, and the babysitting ad one of our boys designed and distributed throughout the neighborhood.) A magazine file holds handfuls of all this paper. Again, when they're packed to capacity, they've got to be cleaned out.

Oversized things like diplomas, large posters and perfect attendance certificates can be stored safely if they are rolled up and put inside paper towel tubes or wrapping paper tubes. The labeled tubes can stand upright in a box for easy access.

Here's a great childproof container that has hundreds of uses — the 9″ × 13″ cake pan with sliding metal lid. These are especially great for traveling and visiting. They hold coloring books, crayons, books, dolls, and lots of things to keep little hands out of mischief. These lap desks also make great cake pans during the off-season, by the way.

Just give each child some kind of container to call his own. These containers are wonderful places for all those stickers kids are always coming up with. Frankly, I would prefer not to have a box under the bed covered with stickers, or drawers full of petrified grasshoppers, but I know I have to make concessions. The rule, "no stickers on walls, windows or furniture" is probably realistic, but kids have to have some breathing room, too. I try to remember to give a little here and there.

OLDIES BUT GOODIES

If you're a wife, you're probably thinking: "Great. But my husband still has his eighth-grade PE shorts. What do I do with them?" Husbands on the other hand are saying, "Here are two

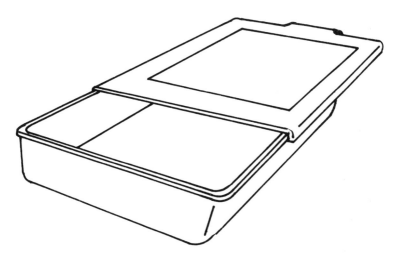

A cake pan with a sliding metal lid makes a great lap desk

unopened cases of *Good Housekeeping* magazines she brought with her when we moved from Chicago in 1958."

There's a little child in all of us, I suppose. We still hang on to old letters and cards, high school yearbooks, cheerleading pom-poms, varsity letters, Clark candy bar wrappers (from an old boyfriend with the same name), and leftover nut cups from the twenty-fifth wedding anniversary party. As parents we are continually bombarded with handmade cards and gifts from the children. You can only display so many things. What then?

The same rules apply to adults and children alike. First, discard and sort. Then, box up, label and store all leftovers in a predesignated, central storage area. (These storage specifics will be covered in a later chapter.)

With an organized plan you and your kids can collect to your heart's content without feeling guilty!

CHAPTER FOURTEEN

Taming the Wild Junk Receptacle

E very home has one: the ever-receptive junk drawer. Here lie the half-dead batteries, a few rubber bands, paper clips, the envelope with Aunt Betty's new address, a safety pin or two, copies of credit card purchases, and maybe a piece of gum. There's the junk drawer, always willing to accept any little morsel that may come its way.

Where is your junk drawer? Is it in the kitchen, in a night stand or end table? What about the family desk? These are the usual places everyone in the family dumps things they can't classify.

In a sense, this catchall seems convenient; you always know where to find the screw that fell out of the toaster. There is always a pencil inside—if the last user remembered to put it back. This is a great place for all those things you don't want to throw away but don't know what to do with. Yes, the junk drawer seems handy and convenient, but is it really?

Actually, the junk drawer is a menace. It looks awful, and there is no system to it. More than likely, when you really need a junk drawer item, it won't be there. If, perchance, a needed something is in the junk drawer, you will probably have to spend several minutes rummaging.

GROUPING IS THE KEY

The key principle when organizing *anything*, from junk drawers to garages, is grouping. Everything in a junk drawer can be categorized. Remove the contents from the drawer and begin: paper clips go into one pile, safety pins into another. Papers necessary for records and needed information should be kept in file folders by subject. Put the buttons with your sewing equipment; the miscellaneous screws where the other screws, nails and tools are kept. Discard whatever you can. Always store things near the point of first use. Gradually you will bring order out of chaos.

In our kitchen we have a "mini office center." Doesn't that sound better than junk drawer? This is a kitchen drawer close to the phone where we keep many needed supplies. Everything in the drawer is compartmentalized so that each item has a well-defined place. Contained in this drawer are two trays I picked up at a discount store in the hair care department. (The trays are made to hold curlers, hair clips and cosmetics.) In the tray compartments we organize pens and pencils, scissors, a paper punch, paper clips, paper clamps, safety pins, rubber bands, stapler and staples, tape, matches, string, screwdriver and scratch pads. Also in this drawer is a mini Rolodex file. This is our name and address directory. Instead of having an address book that needs to be recopied from time to time, we keep all the information on Rolodex cards. There's room on each card to write down the things we want to remember (the names of friends' children, directions to their houses, birthdays, anniversaries, and even our Christmas card list). When someone moves or we need to make a new entry, we simply write a new card for the file. That way, everything stays in alphabetical order.

I use the address file in other ways, too. For example, I can't remember the name of the man we buy tools from, so I have a card labeled *tools*. The man's name, address and phone number are listed on the card. There's a card for television repair filed under *T*, a card for washer repair filed under *W*. The plumber, whose name escapes me, is filed under *P*. If your memory is better than mine, this system won't be necessary. If not, welcome to the club. (Sometimes I staple business cards right to the file card itself, rather than recopying all the information.)

This mini office center is not in a large drawer, but it is neatly organized and extremely useful. Locating it by the phone makes it especially convenient. Keeping these supplies in the kitchen is handy because the kitchen always seems to be the center of activity.

If you do not have a drawer available for these useful supplies, you can hang a pocketed shoe bag or other pocketed organizer to keep the things you need within reach. A tool or tackle box is already divided into sections and can be used as a portable office center. A cash box is another alternative. The added feature here is that the boxes can be locked. One family keeps their supplies in a cardboard shoe box. They call it their useful box, and it is useful—they have one on each floor of their home.

Another alternative is to pick up a parts cabinet. This type of chest, available at discount stores in the tool department, is filled with plastic drawers. (It was designed to hold screws, nuts, bolts and other small pieces.) The chest can sit in a cupboard, be put on an open shelf, or be mounted on a wall. The units are available in various sizes with different numbers and sizes of drawers.

We do have a larger office area in our home where office supplies are stored and records are filed. But having the mini office handy and available saves much time and many unnecessary steps.

Whatever organization option you choose, remember that a junk drawer or mini office will not stay neat and tidy all by itself. Quietly reinforce your newfound organization by quickly replacing misplaced items. Remove the things that do not belong and put them with their categories. It only takes seconds to maintain, but hours to clean!

Take a deep breath, swallow hard and swear off junk drawers forever.

UTILIZING THE UTILITY CLOSET

I hate to sound relentless, but there may be another junk receptacle in or near your kitchen. If you have a utility closet you have probably noticed that it's used as a dumping ground from time to time.

The same principles apply here as applied to the junk drawer. Classify and put away any of the contents that don't belong in the utility closet. Hang up as many things as you can. Things such as your broom, mop, dustpan, fly swatter, vacuum hose, yardstick and bucket can all be hung up and out of the way. If your broom or mop is not equipped with a hook or something you can hang it with, you can always put a screw eye into the end of the handle and hang it on a hook or nail. Drill a hole through the handle or buy the device that snaps onto the end of the stick. Use your imagination. You can usually think of a way to hang (or store) anything.

A pocketed shoe bag can be hung up to hold bottles of cleaners, spray cans, vacuum attachments, or what have you. If you

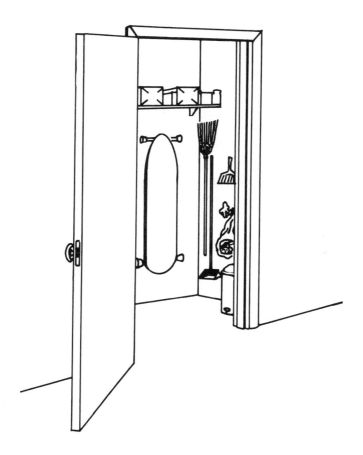

Keep your utility closet organized using the four storage options

don't use the vacuum attachments too often, a drawstring bag can be hung and used to hold them. Don't forget to include extra belts, bags, and the instruction booklet.

A pocketed purse file can be hung up to hold large phone books, grocery sacks, plastic wrap and aluminum foil.

And if you choose not to hang your cache of frequently used cleaning supplies, store them in a clean-up caddy. That keeps everything organized, ready to go, and easy to tote when you're set to clean. Yet if you just want to grab the window cleaner, it's still handy.

Shelf storage is an obvious alternative that can also be used to keep the closet neatly organized. When storing several objects on a shelf, remember to confine them in a box or dishpan so they can be handled as one unit.

Ice cube bins (or other suitable containers) help to categorize and organize the closets' contents. I have one filled with the vacuum belts, bags and filters, one filled with light bulbs, and another with potpourri supplies.

If you have enough room, you should keep a small toolbox in the utility closet. In my toolbox I have a hammer, a few screwdrivers, a small box of assorted nails, tacks, picture hangers, a tape measure, string and scissors. When we have to make a quick repair or hang up a picture, it's so much more convenient to use these nearby supplies than it is to traipse out to the garage.

No matter what shape your closet is in now, you can discard, sort and classify its contents. Then, using some creative storage alternatives, you can work wonders!

CHAPTER FIFTEEN

The Paper Chase

T he biggest threat to a well-ordered home is paper, piles and piles of paper! There are cancelled checks, bank statements, tax records, newspapers, coupons, deeds, loan payment books, sweepstakes notices, directions for cleaning the drapes, lists of service center locations for the Weed Eater, and pamphlets, such as "The Care and Feeding of a Gerbil." This blizzard of paper could chill the nerves of Robocop.

One woman wrote to tell me, "Sometimes I envy people who have disasters and have everything swept away." I know how she feels. Sometimes I've felt like the paper alone could sweep me away.

A PLACE FOR THE PAPER CHASE

A system for handling paper is an absolute necessity. But, before you can have an effective method, you need to establish a well-defined place in your home in which to conduct the family business.

Ideally, of course, a home office would be located in a separate room with a desk, telephone, filing cabinet and typewriter or computer. Though the ideal is not always possible, no matter what your circumstances might be it is possible to have an adequate office center. If a whole room is not available, perhaps there's a small corner tucked away somewhere that would serve the purpose.

First, you will need a surface to write on. This can be a table or a desk. A slab of wood or a hollow-core door laid across the top of two filing cabinets can provide you with a perfectly functional home office desk.

Failing that, you can use a portable, metal filing case (or cardboard box) to hold your files and a tool or tackle box to hold your office supplies. When you're ready to work, you can carry these two essentials to your kitchen and work on the kitchen table.

A paper handling system also requires a place for storing your files. Filing cabinets (usually two drawers are sufficient), cardboard boxes, expanding files, metal, portable filing cases, or under-the-bed boxes are all possibilities.

You will also need some basic supplies:

- Unruled paper and envelopes
- Carbon paper
- Dictionary
- File folders
- Paper clips
- Pencil sharpener
- Pens and pencils
- Rubber bands
- Ruler
- Scissors
- Cellophane tape
- Stamps
- Your calendar or complete planning notebook

A typewriter, computer, telephone and a calculator would be very convenient, but they are not necessary.

It's important to know where everything is. Keep your supplies close to your files and writing surface so you won't have to chase back and forth looking for something you need.

ORGANIZING A HOME FILING SYSTEM

Now, let's put our home office center to use. You should keep three home files (in addition to a safe deposit box at your local bank). These three files are:

1. Active File
2. Dead File
3. Permanent Reference File

The Active File contains material of specific and current interest to the family. These are the papers that keep the family running smoothly (so the water isn't turned off, the IRS is happy, and you can find the manual for the air conditioner when it goes on the blink).

The Dead File contains tax working papers (bill receipts, bank statements, cancelled checks) over three years old.

The Permanent Reference File is for articles, poems, stories, newspaper clippings, craft patterns and music. This file is for things you want to keep indefinitely to refer to and enjoy.

Your safe deposit box should contain the following documents:

1. Birth certificates
2. Citizenship papers
3. Marriage certificates
4. Adoption papers
5. Divorce decrees
6. Wills
7. Death certificates
8. Deeds
9. Titles to automobiles
10. Household inventory
11. Veteran's papers
12. Bonds and stock certificates
13. Important contracts, leases, patents, copyrights and other papers that serve as proof of ownership

WANTED: DEAD OR ALIVE

Let me describe how I use my active and dead files to manage all the paperwork that comes into our home.

In the front of my Active File I have fifteen file folders: Financial, To Do, To File, and one for each month of the year.

Behind these are folders with various subject headings. Some ideas are: Employment records (résumés, letters of recommendation, previous employers, health benefit information), current health benefit information, credit card information, insurance policies, wills (copies), health records, education information (schools attended, degrees, awards, activities, transcripts), safe deposit box inventory (and extra key), record club, car information, services (lawn care, plumber, paper hanger, electrician, building contractor), amusement parks (tickets left over from

Disneyland), scouting information, restaurants (menus for take-out and other information), store or product information, and whatever is of interest to you.

In the back of the Active File, I have an *A* to *Z* expanding file that holds instruction booklets, warranties (the receipts for the products are stapled right to the warranty), appliance manuals, and other product information. The stereo booklet is filed under *S*, the refrigerator manual is filed under *R*, how to clean the drapes is filed under *D* and so on. These things are used so seldom they do not require more detailed filing.

The Financial folder holds anything that has to do with money that has not been taken care of: unpaid bills, bank statements you want to reconcile, credit card receipts you want to check against the bill, magazine renewal forms, and payment and loan booklets.

The To-Do folder holds paper that you have to keep and take action on: a letter you have to answer, a form you need to fill out, a cartoon you want to send to your friend the next time you write to her, tickets to a concert that's coming up in a month.

The information in the To File folder is exactly that. Anything that needs to be placed in a specific file folder can be put in here until you have a chance to file it away. You should file things immediately, but most of us don't want to or don't have time. Things should not be left in this folder, though, for more than a month. If you let it collect for longer than that the job is going to get bigger and bigger, and you're going to procrastinate about doing it. If you can force yourself to do the filing once a month, you will be amazed at how well you're able to stay on top of the paperwork. For simplicity, file things under the broadest possible subject. Use the Active File list for possible categories.

More paper for your files arrives through the mail and other sources. You receive things of interest to other people in the family: personal letters, information about your son's upcoming football camp, notice of a ground beef sale from the butcher, *Sports Illustrated* and other publications. Designate one spot to put this incoming mail, so everyone in the family always knows where to look for it. (Or put it in their in/out baskets.) If you want to keep it out of sight, designate a drawer (be careful here), file folder or basket to hold this miscellaneous material. As soon as possible, get these things into the mainstream of the paper handling process. (When a decision about football camp is reached, schedule it on your calendar, send in the registration form, and get rid of that piece of paper.)

Schedule an hour or so each week to handle paper. As soon as the mail arrives, decide what to keep and what to discard. Do not keep anything that is not currently of interest to someone in your family, even if it might come in handy someday. (Ask yourself, "What will happen if I throw this away?") Quickly put each item into its proper folder. If something needs to be taken care of before your next office session, note it on your calendar, so it won't be forgotten.

The Financial folder is handled in a very simple manner. After you have paid a bill, retain the stub for your records, and place it in the current month's folder. For example, you would put January statements in the January folder, and so on. After you have reconciled your January bank statement, put it in the January folder.

What could be easier? So many times we make our systems so complicated and precise they seem to invite piling up and procrastination. I've had people tell me, "I really like my system. It's different from yours but I really like it. I haven't had time to get to it lately, but when it's working, I sure like it!" If your system is not simple enough to keep up with, you've made it too complicated.

You don't need to have a folder for every company you do business with, and you don't need to sort out tax information every month (unless you really want to).

Records need to be reviewed at least once a year, so you can discard things you no longer need. January is a good month for this job because tax time is just around the corner. Have a tax session to sort out and categorize your tax deductions. Then, discard the following:

1. Salary statements (after you check them against your W-2 form).
2. Cancelled checks for cash or nondeductible items (Note: If you have cancelled checks for large purchases you may want to keep them for insurance purposes).
3. Expired warranties.
4. Expired coupons.
5. Other things no longer needed.

After the tax return is completed, I put the following into a large manila envelope:

1. Paid bill receipts
2. Bank statements
3. Cancelled checks
4. Other tax working papers

The envelope is dated (year ending) and filed in back of the active file. When the envelope is three years old, I take it out and move it to the dead file. Check with your attorney or accountant. You actually may be able to discard these things. The Dead File is seldom used and can be stored in your storage area or some other out-of-the-way place.

Shortly after the first of the year, then, your monthly financial folders should be empty and ready to use for another year. The rest of your active file should be current and in continual use.

PERMANENT REFERENCE FILE

I love to save useful bits of information: decorating tips, information on drug and alcohol abuse, needlework and craft patterns, holiday ideas and activities, exercise and physical fitness information, sheet music, pictures for visual teaching aids and school reports—I could go on forever. I also love to be able to find one of these aids when I want it.

The simplest way to store and retrieve all this information is to put your assorted collection into file folders labeled by subject, then filed alphabetically. For example, all photography articles are put into a folder labeled Photography. When a new article on photography is clipped out, pop it into the Photography folder. This is the beginning of your permanent reference file.

Here's how to get started. Gather all your collected materials and confine them in a box. Now, sit down with a stack of file folders and pick up the first item you're going to file. Let's say it's an article about the ozone layer. Take a file folder and label the tab Environment and put the ozone layer article inside. Now, go on to the next item. You can work in this fashion for a few minutes a day if you need to. But, as long as you chip away at it, the job will gradually (and almost painlessly) be completed. Since the project is confined, you won't have to deal with a mess while you're in the process of filing.

Here are a few helpful hints. When you're setting up your files, it helps to make a file index. For example, when you file the ozone article and make out an environment folder, write Environment on your index. When you set up the photography file, write Photography on the index. After you've established several file folders, your index will begin to take shape and become very useful. Here's how. Let's pretend that you have several file folders in your reference file and you come across an article called "How to Select the Best Camera for You." You clip out the article and decide to put it in your file. Scan the file index to see if you have a file already established where it could logically be placed (Photography). Getting into the habit of checking the index will prevent redundancy (i.e., folders for Photography, Cameras and Pictures).

A helpful rule to remember for labeling your folders is to use nouns, not adjectives. For example, if you have a collection of cute party ideas and file them under *C* for Cute, pretty soon you're going to forget the word cute. Use the noun—parties.

Also, never file paper clips. Paper clips have a way of catching things and can move papers to illogical, hard-to-find locations.

If your reference collection is extensive and you use it frequently, you might benefit from using a numerical filing system. To receive step-by-step instructions for this method, just send me a long, self-addressed, stamped envelope, and I'll be happy to send them to you. Write to P.O. Box 214, Cedar Rapids, IA 52406.

PERIODICALS

Any self-respecting treatise on paper has to include at least a few remarks about magazines and newspapers.

You know what I'm going to suggest, don't you? You're right. Rip out and file the things you want to save, and get rid of the magazines. They can be recycled or donated to hospitals, nursing homes, beauty shops, barber shops, dentists or doctors offices, or any place where people have to wait. Some public libraries offer a magazine trading service. You bring in your old magazines and take home any others that you want.

Libraries store back issues of most magazines and each year the magazines publish an index that the libraries have available. I've been able to find articles that are ten years old. Why should

Confessions of an Organized Homemaker

Periodical Persuasion

Here are three more reasons why you needn't save magazines.

1. Magazines that accept advertising are approximately 80% advertising. Why waste your time and space with that?

2. I've been around long enough to notice that magazines are cyclical. Seems like every few years you read slightly different versions of the same articles.

3. Technological articles and articles about medicine and nutrition are obsolete very quickly nowadays.

---

you put up with the clutter when the library saves and organizes magazines for you?

I know there are stubborn folks who just won't get rid of all their magazines (even I keep some around). Designate a large basket, shelf or drawer (we use an old, antique box) in which to store magazines. When the container is full, you need to get rid of some before you save anymore.

Magazine files (available at discount or office supply stores) hold a year's worth of magazines, but you need shelf space for storage. There are magazine holders you can purchase at office supply stores. They slip into the magazine so it can be stored in a looseleaf binder. Many magazine savers tell me that they staple an index card to the top corner of the magazine cover and jot down the items and page numbers they want to refer to.

Even if you keep magazines, don't let them stagnate. Out with the old and in with the new!

Newspapers should be handled pretty much the same way. My husband reads three newspapers a day, so we'd be buried if we didn't keep up with them. We have a recycle bin in the garage and every day (or at least three times a week) we put all the papers in that bin. Then about once every six or eight weeks, we take the papers to the recycling center. This system really works well for us, because it keeps the mess out of the house. Should we want an item we forgot to clip out, we just go out to the recycle bin and find it.

If you have a backlog of magazines and newspapers, my best advice is to get rid of it *now*, and don't let it get out of control again. For the fainthearted, though, put a handful of magazines in your car and browse through them during minutes of waiting time. If you just can't keep up with all this reading material, save yourself some money, and quit getting it in the first place!

HOUSEHOLD INVENTORY

If you've ever been the victim of a fire or burglary, then you already know the value of having a household inventory. The inventory shows what you possess and how much it is worth. An inventory may also show that you do not have adequate insurance to cover the value of your possessions.

A simple way to make an inventory is to use a tape recorder or video recorder. As you enter each room in your house (don't forget the attic, basement and garage), start at a certain point and move around the room in a circle. Speak into the microphone and say exactly what each object in the room is, how much it cost when it was purchased, and how much it would cost to replace it. Be sure to include serial numbers, model numbers, brand names, dealers' names, and descriptions of the articles. (Many people take pictures of their possessions, thus eliminating some of the description process. Expensive items such as silver, gold and jewelry require close-up photographs.) Check with your insurance agent for your company's exact requirements. If you wish, you can transcribe your taped recording onto paper.

Update your inventory every six months by adding new purchases, or make deletions and indicate new replacement costs (if possible). You may want to type two copies of your tape recording, or perhaps you will choose to write your inventory initially. Whatever method you use, an inventory may be very useful to you. Keep one copy of it in your safe deposit box.

Finally, make a record of where all your important papers are located. A loose-leaf binder (filed in your Active File) is a good place for this information. For added security, though, you might want to put a copy in the safe deposit box or fireproof safe.

What to include:

1. List of all bank accounts
2. Where safe deposit box is located
3. All family members' social security numbers

4. Insurance policy numbers and agents' names
5. Copy of household inventory
6. Record of household improvements

This system isn't necessary, but some type of system is. Whatever method you use, make sure that someone else in your family knows and understands it.

CHAPTER SIXTEEN

How to Organize Another Person

Who is this paragon of virtue, this man of steel, who is able to bend wire in his bare hands (and throw the scraps into the junk drawer)? This man of might, disguised as a husband, is more powerful than a locomotive (when he's hauling things home from the dump); able to leap tall piles of dirty clothes in a single bound (when he's heading for the golf course); and faster than a speeding bullet (when it's time for a ball game).

The question I am asked over and over is, "How can I organize my husband?" First, you must realize that is a difficult question. There are men out there who still have the hubcaps from their first cars!

Men aren't the only offenders, though. Many men have complained to me about all the junk their wives have hoarded. One man called to say, "For years my wife blamed everything on the kids. Now the kids are gone and the house is still a wreck. She saves everything."

One woman always bragged that it didn't make any difference to her husband how the house looked. All the confusion didn't bother him one little bit! One evening this woman gathered her family around her and passed out a sheet of paper to each one. She innocently asked everyone to list the goals they had for themselves and for the family. When the papers were passed back, she was surprised by her husband's responses. Everything on his list had to do with bringing more order, organization and peace into their home!

I know of one man who solved his junk accumulation problem by building a storage area in the rafters over his garage. That, he thought, would pacify his wife. It did, for a while, until the roof over the garage began to give way. His wife was almost delighted thinking now he would surely have to dispose of his collection.

Never fear, this Metropolis Marvel outwitted his wife! Armed with several two-by-fours he propped up the roof and (just in the knick of time) saved his treasures from obliteration.

Obviously, some people are resourceful (and stubborn) little devils who are bound and determined to collect and stash their trash. In many cases it does cause frustration and disharmony at home.

Organizing other people is the only area where I can't guarantee success, but I know four simple rules that will help.

RULE NUMBER ONE: SET AN EXAMPLE

Unfortunately, one of the first rules of organization is: You cannot organize another person. You can, however, set a good example. Sometimes when people begin to see the amounts of time and money saved through an organizational program, they begin to follow suit. Patience is the major factor here.

Chances are when you undertake an organizational project everyone in the family is going to think you're going through a stage that will soon pass. More than likely, they will ignore any attempts on your part to get things into shape. It's only when you hang in there and your efforts pass the test of time that they will realize you mean business.

Above everything else, don't play the martyr. Trust me. I've tried. It doesn't work. Now, when I start feeling woebegone and wretched, wallowing in self-pity, I just gather up an armload of junk to put away and say to myself, "I'm doing this for *me*." I'm happier, more energetic, and have more free time when the house is tidy.

Many times when I'm busily involved in something, one of the kids will ask me to fix them a snack—a sandwich or a bowl of cereal or something. Almost without exception I tell the child to just help himself. In other words I tell my child, if you're the one that wants it, you do the work. The same thing sort of applies to household organization. If it's extremely important to you, then you're going to have the bulk of the responsibility. Now, I'm not suggesting that you carry the burden alone. I'm just giving you some self-pity repellent.

RULE NUMBER TWO: TALK IT OVER

Tell your spouse *once* that it is important to you to have a smoothly running system. Saying it more than once constitutes nagging and will cause further discord.

One wife complained that her husband always put kitchen utensils away in the wrong place. One day she told him that she had designated certain places for each gadget. She further explained to him that the things were there for a reason. As soon as he saw the logic behind her system, he cooperated. So tell your mate once, and see what happens.

Get Everyone Involved

Tell the children what you're doing. Ask for their ideas. They love to feel that they're part of things, and they'll be more willing to cooperate.

After planting his garden, our neighbor was worried about the rowdy little boy who lived next door to him. He was afraid the boy would tromp through the plants and destroy the crops. This man decided to make the child a part of the project. "Freddy," he said, "I've just planted my garden. I'm afraid that the neighbor children will run through it and ruin it. Will you help me guard these plants?" Freddy rose to the occasion and watched those plants like a professional security guard.

So, draw the kids into the project by asking for their help and ideas.

Try a Tradeoff

Tell him if he'll hang up his clothes, you'll take out the garbage. Tell her you'll change diapers if she'll weed the garden. Discuss which chores are most distasteful to each of you, and see if a tradeoff is possible. This can work with children, too!

Be Understanding

There are probably certain things that you do that are irritating. Giving and taking is what a good relationship is all about. What may seem like a worthless trinket may be as valuable to your spouse as the car is to you.

RULE NUMBER THREE: MAKE IT CONVENIENT

Convenience is extremely important when trying to unclutter another person. If you are using the principle of giving things a well-defined, well-confined place, you have already brought much convenience into your home.

The family has to relearn where things belong and they won't always cooperate. But if you persist and keep returning things to their well-defined places, eventually the family will join forces with you. They will have a clear vision in their minds where things belong, rather than a vague idea.

Our youngest son often played Superman or Batman and needed to wear a cape. He would go into the bathroom and select just the right towel. Then he'd get a safety pin to secure his costume. Every time he wanted a safety pin, he knew exactly where to get one. They are always where they are supposed to be. When he was finished playing superhero and I asked him to put the safety pin back, he knew exactly where it belonged.

Be sure family members see that your improvements are saving time, energy, and sometimes money.

When our children were younger, each one had a dishpan on the floor of his closet to hold his shoes. Their shoes were small, so even though they had several different pairs, they all fit nicely into the dishpan. We seldom had to look for shoes because they had a well-defined, convenient place.

If someone is constantly dropping clothes where they were taken off, ask the person if they'll at least put them all in the same corner or on the same chair. Whoever picks up the mess will have it all in one place instead of every place.

Put a basket on top of a dresser or on the refrigerator (or wherever) to hold business cards, keys, change and miscellaneous tidbits that come home in pockets or purses. Instead of having this stuff thrown on the table, it can be out of sight in a decorative basket. (To avoid turning this catch-all into a junk drawer, clean it out every few days.)

If your collector isn't using certain things and still refuses to get rid of them, box them up and store these boxes in a storage area. Put the person's name and the date on the box. The offender will have the security of knowing the belongings are safe and close at hand. Chances are that in six years, when they see the date on the box, they will see the folly of their ways and give things away. One woman has several boxes in her basement: Hank's box No. l, Hank's box No. 2, Hank's box No. 3 . . .

For often-used items, be sure storage is convenient. If family members have to go upstairs (or downstairs) to put the glue and scissors away, then they probably won't. They'll just stick the scissors in a handy spot and you'll have to look for them the next time you want them.

Think of the things lost or misplaced most often and ask yourself these questions:

1. Where is this item mostly used?
2. Do I keep this in a convenient place?
3. Does it have a well-defined place?
4. Do I need more than one? (Example: one pair of scissors upstairs and one downstairs.)

People often ask me why the glue and scissors (or whatever) are always where they are supposed to be in our house. One reason is that we usually use glue, for example, in two rooms: the kitchen and a downstairs room next to the family room. So I keep two sets of these things, one set in each room. When the glue is used in the kitchen, it stays in the kitchen, even though it may not be put back into the drawer where it belongs. (To be honest, our kids don't put things away any better than anyone else's kids do.) So, store things where people use them, keep them in a convenient, well-defined place, and if you *really* need to duplicate items to maintain order, do so. Even if family members don't put the item away, at least it'll be left in the room in which it belongs.

Try to be persistent. When you find a safety pin, put it where it belongs. When you find a pencil, put it away. Soon everyone will see the rewards of order—no more looking and searching. Everything will be found when it's needed. Impatience and irritation will not be as frequently felt or expressed. Gradually they'll come to realize that your improvements are saving time, energy, and money. Convenience will teach family members that order gives much more pleasure than disorder.

RULE NUMBER FOUR: PRAISE

As a motivator, nothing works like sincere praise. When things are messed up after all your hard work, refrain from criticism.

That will only cause more resistance. A good measure of praise for jobs well done will get much better results.

One night after dinner our oldest boy picked up his dishes and brought them over to the sink. After picking myself up from a dead faint, I complimented him on his thoughtfulness. But I didn't stop there. I told everyone that I had a boy who brought his dishes to the sink after eating.

One evening his teacher called me to tell me that they were celebrating his birthday in school the next day. She wanted to know a few things about him—his favorite color, favorite food, a good habit, etc. You can be sure I told her his good habit and she announced it to his whole class the next day. Even though that was several years ago, Jim is still bringing his dishes to the sink. He has to live up to his reputation.

Don't forget appreciation and praise works for teenagers and adults, too. Express gratitude for every little contribution someone makes. My husband frequently does the dishes and always puts things away wherever the mood strikes him. So, I usually have to spend a few minutes the next day putting things back where they belong. I always thank him for his help and don't criticize or complain about the way things are put away. I always remind myself that he's saved me forty-five minutes or so by doing the dishes. Why should I fuss about two or three minutes spent reorganizing?

If you do find it necessary to correct or criticize, try the "sandwich" principle. Simply stated, that is a bad remark sandwiched between two good remarks. Sometimes it's been so bad around here I've had to say, "The ceiling in here looks great! You really need to get rid of this junk on the floor, though. I'm happy to see one of your shoes in the shoebag." Anyway, I'm sure you get the idea. Just find two good points even if you have to stretch it a bit, and sandwich a bad one in between.

Try these four simple rules. I can't promise anything, but I'm sure you'll at least see an improvement.

There's one more problem we haven't covered—the problem of undoing a hard day's work.

THE BEST REASON TO GET ORGANIZED

After I gave a lunch-and-learn lecture at the IRS, a member of the audience asked me: "I know I can go home and do all of

---

HOW TO ORGANIZE ANOTHER PERSON

I've found these tactics as successful with adults as with children:

1. *Set an example.* If you have everything precisely how you want it, neat and orderly, wouldn't anyone else want the same?

2. *Talk it over.* Sometimes the direct approach is best.

3. *Try a tradeoff.* "If you make dinner this week, I'll reorganize your work shed."

4. *Be understanding.* Some people have a much harder time with organization than others.

5. *Praise.* Positive reinforcement works wonders.

---

this. I also know that in one week, I'll have to do the whole thing over. What can I do?"

Another question that often arises is, "What do you do when you've spent all day cleaning and the kids come home and undo everything in five minutes?" In the interest of space, I will try to condense my remarks. I believe there are entire books written on this subject. I know the frustrations that are borne out of this situation, because I have felt them also. I feel strongly, though, that herein lies the greatest reason in the world to get organized.

If you are only a surface cleaner, then the children really are undoing all your hard work. It is difficult and time-consuming to clean and maintain order when things under the surface are not in tip-top shape. When the kids undo, you really are at point zero—again. No wonder we suffer from frustration and depression.

Imagine for a minute that you live in a home that is clutter-free. Everything in the home has a well-defined, well-confined place. Cleaning an already orderly home is twice as fast and half as fatiguing. The kids come home from school, drop their coats and boots in the corner, throw their papers and books on the counter, grab a snack, spill the milk, drop crumbs on the floor, and so on. Sure, the surface is getting messed up, but underneath it all there is still peace and order. Cupboards, closets and drawers are still neat and tidy. Things can still be found and put away quickly. In a home such as this, bringing the surface under control is not really a big deal.

Organization does not take the place of discipline. Kids still need to be given rules and guidelines for behavior. Let your children know what is expected of them, and before the situation is really out of control, start controlling it. Protect your investment by spending a few minutes to regain a semblance of order. If you delegate, follow through. If you do it yourself, don't complain.

Remember, how long does it really take to straighten up an organized, orderly home? Not long at all! Believe me, the road to getting organized is the road to better mental health.

Whatever course of action you take, don't let your desire for order ruin your marriage or your family life. Next time you are faced with another mess, step back, take a deep breath, and say to yourself, "This is the signature of someone I love!"

CHAPTER SEVENTEEN

Interruptions — The Hidden Destroyers

Housework is more subject to interruptions than any other field of human endeavor. Is it any wonder we sometimes want to get away from it all? How we long to lock the world out and bask in the sunshine of uninterrupted time.

While this is a delightful fantasy, we all need to realize that a certain number of interruptions are to be expected. However, many interruptions are not necessary and can be skillfully eliminated. We need to learn how to work in spite of them. One important principle I still struggle with is this: Don't let an imperfect situation be an excuse to do nothing. Interruptions will never go away, so don't wait for them to disappear before you start something.

What are the hidden interruptions in your life? One easy way to determine what (or who) the time-destroyers are is to spend a few minutes at the end of the day thinking about where your time went. Jot down the little irritations and interruptions that obstructed your progress. Quickly note how your time was spent. After several days you may notice a trend. What problems keep recurring?

You may feel that spending a few minutes a day analyzing your time expenditure is asking a little much. However, if you are feeling unfulfilled and frustrated, it is necessary for you to do this. The result of getting control over your time will be greater freedom. You can spend all day putting out fires, or you can catch the guy with the matches — the choice is yours.

Another thing you can try is to jot down each interruption as it occurs, noting who the interrupter was, when it happened and what was needed. This makes for a slightly chopped-up day, but it is a very effective short-term exercise. When done for four or five days, it will give you a clear indication of what is happening to your time and who the chief offender is.

You may discover that many of your interruptions are caused by someone not being able to find something. Perhaps there is not an adequate laundry routine and lack of desired clothing is causing problems. Maybe meals are not well planned and prepared, causing constant eating and unscheduled trips to the store. Be honest with yourself and identify those time robbers. Knowing the cause of your problems will lead to the solutions.

Many times we cause our own problems. If you're really frustrated with your lack of time and feel as if you never get anything accomplished, you need to take more drastic measures. I don't usually recommend this, because most people won't follow through with it. However, it is a very revealing project that can put you on track. The method is simple. Keep a log of your entire day in fifteen-minute increments. Do this consistently for four or five days, and you will learn a lot about yourself and your family.

After doing this activity myself, I thought it was kind of fun, and it opened my eyes. I always hated changing sheets on the bed. But after keeping this time chart, I discovered it only took two or three minutes for this job. Now, I don't mind changing sheets at all.

This chart will tell you how much time you spend sleeping, eating, reading, watching TV, talking on the phone, and how long it takes to clean the bathroom. You will have a bird's-eye view of where your time goes. You may even surprise yourself and see that you are accomplishing a great deal more than you thought. The chart will also tell you if you're too busy and need to say no more often. You may see a need for more delegation — there are many things to be done, but where is it written that *you* have to do them all?

Your attitude about interruptions is also important. Solve the problems you can solve. (For example, buy a pump and filter for the fishbowl so you won't have to change the water so often.) Then change your attitude about the problems you can't solve. When the phone rings tell yourself that chatting for a minute is a nice change of pace. "The pause that refreshes" sounds less irritating than "interruption." When the kids or your spouse

	MON.	TUES.	WED.	THURS.	FRI.
8:00					
:15					
:30					
:45					
9:00					
:15					
:30					
:45					
10:00					
:15					
:30					
:45					
11:00					
:15					
:30					
:45					
12:00					

Use a chart like this for a couple of days to see where interruptions are most prevalent interrupt your activities, you can choose to think of it as an inconsiderate act or as a moment to teach, listen and show love.

HOW TO HANDLE PHONE INTERRUPTIONS
Let's talk about some specific ways to handle these insidious time-robbers. But first you must know that time management is a very personal matter. We can't all use the same techniques, because we all have different personalities. What works for one person will not work for another.

Most everyone ranks the telephone as archenemy number one as far as interruptions are concerned. A lot of people take the phone off the hook, unplug it, or turn on the answering machine. Some folks with nerves of steel let the phone ring.

One woman I know keeps her phone off the hook every morning until ten or until her top priority tasks are completed. Her friends soon learn when the best time is to catch her, and they call her later. She eliminates phone solicitors and bill collectors during her high priority time. Her attitude about emergencies is that there are other ways to be contacted, and if it's important enough, she'll be reached.

If you do pick up the phone, it may be difficult to put down. But there are ways to end a telelphone conversation. Develop one that suits your personality. For example, I know of one man who ends phone conversations by saying lightheartedly, "Well, I'm getting tired of talking to you." Or, "I'm getting bored with this whole conversation." With his particular personality it comes off great, and he gets away with it. However, you couldn't get me to try it!

Throughout the suggestions that follow, try to pick up some ideas that you are comfortable with, and see if your telephone interruption problem can at least be mitigated.

If you enjoy your phone calls and your clean house, as you're cleaning, you can do your kitchen last. Whenever the phone rings, answer it in the kitchen, and clean as you talk. When the conversation is over, return to where you were when the phone rang, and get back to your original job. If the phone rings often enough, the whole kitchen can be done in what would have been wasted time.

Another idea is to keep a craft or other project in a covered basket by the phone. Whenever the phone rings, use it as a signal to work on your project. Crocheting, knitting, embroidery, cross-stitch, needlepoint, mending and ironing are all good phone projects. Besides, you'll be surprised how fast something can be completed when you chip away at it regularly.

We've all read lists of things you can do while talking on the phone: fold and mend clothes, iron, straighten drawers and cupboards, clean stoves, refrigerators, wipe down a wall and do your nails (to name a few). These are good ideas, and telephone shoulder rests will allow you to use both hands freely while you're talking. But one important option is always omitted from these lists and that is simply to sit down and enjoy the call. There really is nothing wrong with sitting down and doing nothing. Relaxation is not a waste of time, providing it isn't your number one priority. We all need to be less compulsive, so we can savor life and each other a little more.

SAYING "NO" TO REQUESTS

If you simply can't say no without feeling uncomfortable, calendaring and scheduling can help painlessly eliminate a lot of problems. Many of us are concerned with outside demands on our time. Always remember that people are more important than programs, and you have to use wise judgement when you say no.

Your first priority is your family and the responsibility you have to the lifestyle you have chosen. If your willingness to help others is really being abused, use your calendar. List the things you want to accomplish, and tell the interrupter you can't squeeze another thing in.

Set firm appointments with yourself to accomplish high priority jobs. Treat such an appointment with the same respect you would if it were an appointment with your lawyer or doctor. If someone calls or in some other way interrupts you and asks you to do something you feel you can't (or shouldn't) handle, tell your friend (or whomever) that you have an appointment and you just can't miss it. Here are a few more miscellaneous tips to help you cut down on other interruptions.

• Have a set time for yourself and make others honor it.
• Give things in your home a well-defined place so you won't be continually interrupted to find things.
• Plan menus carefully so all ingredients are on hand. (Hide

especially tempting ingredients so they'll be there when you need them.)

• Stock up on birthday party presents, wrapping paper and cards, and save many trips to the store.

• Hang a note on the front door when you don't want to be disturbed.

• When playing chauffeur, do grocery shopping, run other errands, or work on a portable project while the kids are taking lessons (or whatever).

• Schedule housekeeping and other projects so you'll have all your supplies handy when you need them.

• Note little annoyances and prepare for them. For example, our youngest child has a passion for milk and he was constantly asking me for some. I started keeping a glass in the refrigerator just for him. Whenever he was thirsty, he could get his own drink without interrupting me.

If you know you're going to be engrossed in a project and you don't want the children to bother you for a while, try this. A half hour or so before you begin the project, read a story to the kids or play a game with them. Gather them around the piano for a songfest. In other words, you're satisfying their immediate need for your attention. Then, when you start your project, they won't feel so desperate for your presence.

Anticipate interruptions and stop them before they start. I remember when our kids were little, as soon as I'd get out the mop to clean the floor, one of them wanted to mop. It happened every time. So, I anticipated the interruption. About fifteen minutes or so before I was ready to mop the floor I'd get out the mop and put a little water in a dishpan. Then one of the kids would start to wash the floor. By the time I was actually ready to take over, the child was bored with the chore and ready to take off.

Another frequent interruption from kids is, "I'm bored." I hear it almost every day. I'm not always successful at combatting this interruption, but I've made progress. Since I know this is going to come up, I try to keep two or three ideas in my mind of suggestions I can make. I used to just say, "Go read." Now, I'm more creative. "Go work on your scrapbook. Make a tissue paper picture. Weave a basket." (Whenever I see an inexpensive

HOW TO HANDLE INTERRUPTIONS

1. Before the interruptor gets into full swing, ask if you can get back to him or her.

2. To avoid phone interruptions, take the phone off the hook.

3. If you have one, let your answering machine handle phone interruptions.

4. Plan ahead and have what you need on hand. (Stock up on cards, gifts and staple food items to avoid last-minute trips.)

5. There are some interruptions that cannot be put off. Learn to anticipate these. Some are very regular.

6. Set aside uninterruptable time for yourself on a regular basis. Others will learn (eventually) to approach you at another time.

or closeout craft kit I'll buy it and save it for just such occasions.) Kits for making baskets, leather accessories, jewelry and hair accessories have proven very helpful. There are also simple kits for cross-stitch, plastic canvas embroidery and fabric painting — you name it.

At the end of every school semester the kids need new school folders and spiral notebooks. I don't know how many times I've been dragged to the store after dinner to get the supplies for the kids. (Of course, every other family was also so engaged, creating added congestion.) The last time I battled the crowds I promised myself, "Never again." Now, I anticipate this interruption and stock up once for a whole year.

As you organize each area of your home and your life, you will have fewer and fewer interruptions. Isn't it exciting to discover that a few basic organizing principles can change your whole life?

PART FOUR

STORAGE

CHAPTER EIGHTEEN

The Story on Storage

W e're nearing the end of our journey. We've planned and uncluttered, filed and fed. If you've done your job well, you should have a lot of things needing to be stored. Only the real necessities should be taking up precious space in your drawers and shelves. Now, what to do with all the leftovers?

First, let's make a last-ditch effort to eliminate as much as possible. Before you store anything, make sure you really need it. There's no sense storing a flash attachment from an old, discarded camera, lids to broken casserole dishes, or two books left from your set of 1947 encyclopedias. Once again, think through your belongings. Do you really need the things you're planning to store?

Before putting anything into storage ask yourself, "What would happen if I got rid of this?" If the answer is "nothing," that should tell you something. Also, ask yourself "How hard would it be to replace this object should I decide to get rid of it?" Using these two questions as guidelines will help you be more objective.

Here are a few different storage methods that have been tried and tested by thousands of people. Read each one and pick the method that seems easiest for you.

No matter which method you choose, you'll need a supply of boxes. Produce boxes (available at most grocery stores) are very sturdy and have lids. The lids are easier to get off if you cut them down so they're approximately five inches deep. You might also want to cut handle holes in the sides of the boxes, so you can grab them more easily when you slide them off the shelf.

Cardboard file boxes are sturdy, inexpensive, and easily found in the office section at discount stores or office supply stores. Computer paper boxes (check computer stores) or paper boxes (from the printer or photocopy place) are good choices.

You can also check the yellow pages under "boxes." Many cities have paper companies that manufacture boxes and will sell them to the public (though you may have to buy them in quantity). Another source to check is places like U-Haul. They have do-it-yourself moving supplies and sell all sizes of sturdy boxes.

There is a variety of plastic storage boxes with lids available at discount stores. These come in many different sizes and colors and will last forever. But they are, naturally, much more expensive than cardboard.

Let's get started.

STORAGE SYSTEM NUMBER ONE

Sort your things into groups. Below are some logical categories that might make sorting easier:

- *Adult.* For adult clothing including maternity clothing.
- *Baby.* For baby clothing through size two and baby equipment.
- *Children.* For children's clothing size three and over and children's shoes.
- *Decorations.* All holiday decorations. If you have a lot of decorations, rather than grouping decorations into one large category, you may prefer to break them down into individual groupings, such as *CH*—Christmas, *HA*—Halloween, *E*—Easter, *V*—Valentines, *T*—Thanksgiving.
- *Furnishings.* Throw rugs, bedspreads, blankets, curtains and decor pieces.
- *Household.* Dishes, gadgets and small appliances, pans.

After your boxes are packed and labeled (just write the contents on the side of the box), code your boxes with permanent marker. The first box of adult clothing is marked *A-1*, the second is marked *A-2* and so on. For this method, use the following code for your major categories: *A*—adult, *B*—baby, *C*—children, *D*—decorations, *F*—furnishings and *H*—household.

Perhaps you will have more or different categories. Simply use the first letter of each category as the code letter. That way, it's easy to remember.

Now let me explain why you code at all. Let's say you want the cornucopia for a centerpiece. Since you use it as a Thanksgiving decoration you know it's going to be in a box labeled *D* for decorations. Go out to your shelves where all the boxes are stored and go right to the *D* boxes. The list of contents on each box quickly tells you which *D* box contains the cornucopia.

Also, if you choose to be very organized, you can make an index card for each of your storage items (or groups of storage items). On the top of the index card you'd write, for example, Cornucopia. Then just under that you'd indicate where the cornucopia is located: D-2.

Another method is to make a list wherein all your storage items and their locations are listed. Then, when you want something, check your list and see where it is stored.

STORAGE SYSTEM NUMBER TWO
Pack all your stored items into boxes and give each box a number. As you're packing the boxes, though, fill out an index card for each item and note which box number it's stored in—snow cone maker, box 3; Boy Scout mess kit, box 9, and so on. Then file the cards in alphabetical order. When you need something, flip through the card file and the index tells you exactly where the desired item is located.

STORAGE SYSTEM NUMBER THREE
This is called the SOS (storage organizing system). This is a purchased system that includes a looseleaf notebook, colored tab dividers, index sheets and colored, numbered box labels. This system is ideal for those who have a lot of things stored that they want to find quickly. Here's how it works. Everything in your home can be divided into as many as ten color-coded categories:

- *Gray.* Bedroom—clothes, accessories, shoes, sheets, bedding.
- *Goldenrod.* Books.
- *Yellow.* Toys.
- *Blue.* Household.
- *Dark Pink.* Kitchen.
- *Tan.* Office and school supplies.
- *Green.* Furnishings and decor.

BOX NO.	CONTENTS
PINK	Crafts and Hobbies
ORCHID	Holiday Decorations
SALMON	Bathroom

- *Pink.* Crafts and hobbies.
- *Orchid.* Holiday decorations.
- *Salmon.* Bathroom.

You might want to change the color key. I use this system, but I only have five categories (adult, children, decorations, household and furnishings).

The SOS has ten sets of color-coded packing labels for your storage boxes. Each section contains enough perforated labels for twenty-five boxes. The SOS also contains index sheets on which you'll list the contents of each box.

Let's pretend you're packing away the Halloween decorations. Flip to the orchid section (orchid is the color for holiday decorations) and then tear off the four orchid labels marked number 1. With clear plastic mailing tape or glue, secure these four labels to the four side panels on your storage box. Next, turn to the index sheets in the orchid section and record the necessary information.

That's all there is to it.

Because the box is labeled on all four sides, it's easy to see at a glance what's in the box. No matter how the box is situated or stacked, the index quickly tells you what's inside the carton. You never have to write the contents of a carton down the side of the box. You never have to open a box to see what's inside. You won't have to lift or turn a box around to read the contents list. Because the system is color coded and categorized, it automatically organizes everything in your home.

The SOS is a good storage option only if you have quite a few boxes (more than ten). For ordering information, call Home Management at 1-800-835-TIME (8463).

SPECIAL TIPS ON CLOTHING STORAGE

Clothing storage is usually a problem, especially where children's apparel is concerned. The longer clothes are stored, the worse they look, so be selective about the things you save. Don't accept hand-me-downs from others if you don't need them.

Perhaps you've had the experience of going through a storage box only to find a great article of clothing you had forgotten about. Now, it's too small for the child. One idea that can help prevent this is to have two storage boxes for each child (whenever practical). One box can hold out-of-season clothes, and one can hold clothes to grow into. As soon as one of your children outgrows a particular outfit, put the clothes into the box of the person who'll wear it next. Go through the boxes every spring and fall taking anything out that the child will wear before the season is over. Another method is to sort things by season, sex and size.

With inexpensive molding (nailed into the studs of all three sides of the closet walls) and particle board, you can build an extra shelf above the installed closet shelf, and store the out-of-season and grow-into boxes right in the child's room. This will create easy storage access using what would otherwise be wasted space.

Get into the habit of going through the clothes twice a year either spring and fall or summer and winter. Pack away the out-of-season clothes and check the grow into box. Don't store anything that the child will not be able to wear next season. Hand it down to another child or otherwise recycle it.

Adult clothing should also be rotated twice a year. Out-of-season clothes should be boxed or hung up out of the mainstream to get them out of the way. Any clothing you haven't worn for a year should be eliminated. Give it away or sell it at a tag sale or consignment shop. If you haven't worn something for a while, there's usually a reason. Is that reason going to change in the immediate future? Probably not.

One of our friends lives in a small house that's short on storage space. So, she got a few large, thirty-gallon plastic garbage cans and stores out of season clothes in those. Instead of using the lids, she placed twenty-four-inch round plywood pieces on top. Then she covered them with decorative, round tablecloths. No one ever guesses that her accent tables are useful storage bins! (Good idea for storing sleeping bags and blankets, too.)

One-motion storage is extremely important to any storage program. Things that are too big to be stored in boxes should be kept in clear plastic bags (when necessary) so they are in full view. Storage shelves that are too wide will force you to store things one in front of the other, thus defeating your one-motion storage goal. If you're stuck with deep shelves, though, just be sure that the cartons that are stored in the front are the ones you're using most often. If cartons are hard to get to or difficult to open, you'll probably start piling things up "for now" with plans to put them into storage boxes later.

Make your system easy to use and easy to get to. It'll cut down on procrastination. Simplify things, make them convenient, and you will be more likely to follow through with your program.

CHAPTER NINETEEN

The Four Storage Options

Did you know that about 10 percent of the space in your home or apartment is needed for storage? That means, if you have a 2,000-square-foot home, you need 200 square feet of storage space available to you. How does your storage space stack up? (Pun intended.)

Many of us complain that we do not have enough room for storage. More than likely, we either have too many things or we have not used our existing space efficiently. Before adding any new storage areas to your home, be sure that you have eliminated unnecessary belongings. Organize the space you have before you undertake any major building projects.

Remember the law of the home: Junk expands to fill the space available, plus one room. More storage space may just give you more space in which to be disorganized.

We are all bound, to some degree, by the architecture of our living quarters. A particular article may seem best suited to drawer storage, but when you have no drawer space you must start using your imagination. There are only four storage options. You can either *hang* things up, store them in a *drawer*, store them on a *shelf*, or put them on the *floor*. If drawer storage, for example, is not possible, ask yourself if the items can be hung, put on a shelf, or stored on the floor in some manner.

No matter what storage problem you are faced with, you can find your best storage alternative by looking at these four possibilities. Oftentimes, you can work around the existing architecture of your home and save the many hours and dollars of a remodeling project. Next time you hear yourself saying, "Now, what am I going to do with this?" stop and think. Then ask yourself, "Of the four storage options (floor, drawer, shelf, hanging) which one would work best for me?"

In the chapters that follow, you will learn how to physically organize the space around you. To give you a stronger foundation on which to build, let's examine each storage option in detail.

HANG IT UP

Here, you have a variety of possibilities. Kitchen utensils are easily adaptable to hanging. Most restaurant kitchens store things in this manner, so it must be an efficient method.

Items can be hung on peg-board or out of sight on the inside of cupboard or closet doors. If you hang the items used most frequently in your kitchen mixing center, you'll save steps in preparing meals.

In the kitchen and bathroom, look under your sinks. There is a lot of wasted space there. Stock buckets or plastic ice cream pails with extra or seldom used things, and hang them on nails. They're out of sight, out of your way, and still accessible when you need them.

There are many commercial products designed to help you hang anything from paper sacks to the ironing board. Even metal parts cabinets (the kind with all the little plastic drawers) can be hung up. If you're unaware of the products available, walk through the housewares and hardware departments in all of your favorite stores. Check industrial or business supply catalogs. Acquaint yourself with the variety of storage helpers you can purchase.

Bats, rackets and other sports equipment can be hung on peg-board or secured between two closely placed nails. Stored in this way they are safe, visible, easy to find, and easy to replace after use. This same system is extremely effective with tools and lawn-care equipment.

Here are a few other hanging ideas: Hang a pocketed shoe bag to hold things like vacuum attachments. Such bags can also hold cleaning supplies, shoes, socks, curling iron, blow dryer, hair spray, hats, scarves, mittens, sewing items, and any number of things.

Cup hooks screwed onto the bottom rod of a wooden coat hanger can hold things such as belts, purses and jewelry. Slip a link of a chain around the neck of a hanger, attach shower curtain hooks every few links, and you've got instant hanging storage for purses, toy bags or what have you. Sew cafe rings to the backs of stuffed animals and hang them up and out of the way. Velcro is another alternative.

Tension rods provide easy hanging storage. Put one up in the doorway while you're ironing and you've got a convenient, temporary place to hang pressed clothing. Tension rods can also be used to hold wide rolls of wrapping paper. (Or snap the rolls into wall mounted clips of the type used to hang brooms or mops.) A tension rod between two closet walls could be used for additional hanging storage in the closet.

Mount a tension rod on the side wall of the clothes' closet between the back wall and the front wall. Hang open, metal shower curtain hooks on the rod, and you've made a convenient holder for belts and purses.

Cover a piece of cardboard with contact paper or wallpaper scrap. Then put on a few rows of self-adhesive cup hooks. This is an extremely handy necklace organizer. You can hang the board in the back of your closet, on the back of a door, or frame it and hang it on the wall.

Low closet rods can greatly increase the amount of available closet space. If you don't want to go to the expense of installing one permanently, for a few dollars a commercial product is available that simply hooks onto the existing rod. Or, even less expensive, make a low closet rod yourself. Here's how: Cut a 1-inch dowel to the desired length. With screws, attach a piece of chain to each end of the dowel. Put a shower curtain ring in the last link of both lengths of the chain. Slip the shower curtain hook over the regular closet rod and snap them shut. You now have a trapeze-type closet rod for a fraction of the cost of a purchased model. (Instead of the wooden dowel, you can substitute a piece of 1-inch PVC pipe. The chain runs down from the original closet rod, through the pipe, and back up to the rod.)

A curtain or towel rod can be hung on the back of a door to hold a bedspread or quilt, table linen, your next day's outfit, jewelry, or ties.

Cup hooks screwed to the underside of a shelf or cupboard can hold belts, tote bags, kitchen utensils, tools, jewelry or even cups.

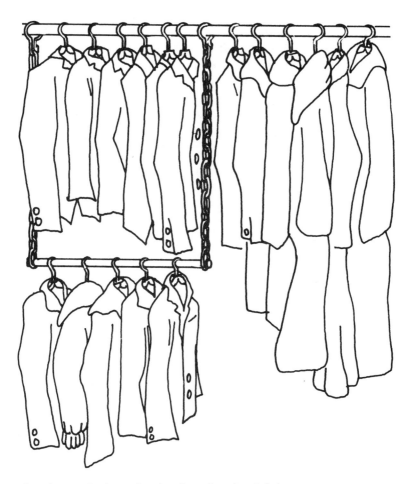

A low closet rod using a dowel and two lengths of chain

Triple-tiered wire baskets (for fruits and vegetables) can hold whatever you can think of, such as beauty supplies (nail polish, lipstick, shampoo or soap) or a few small stuffed animals.

As you can see, hanging is one of the most versatile of the four storage alternatives. Use it and see how much space opens up for you.

STORE IT ON THE FLOOR

Here are a few ideas to get you started. When it comes to the floor, don't ignore the space between things. This is especially evident in the kitchen. Do you have a space between the refrigerator and the counter? What about the space between other appliances? These spots are ideal for large trays, cookie sheets, cutting boards, etc. Start inspecting your rooms and notice those small inconspicuous places.

Look under things. Everyone is familiar with covered, under-the-bed boxes that are widely available. An old drawer with casters under each corner can provide ample, rolling storage under a bed. A long dust ruffle under a crib or table can hide a large storage area that would otherwise be unused or cluttered.

A closet floor may have storage potential. Stacking vegetable bins can hold shoes or folded sweaters. A wastebasket kept on a closet floor can hold hangers—no more pushing clothes back and forth to locate one. And, when washday rolls around, the hangers are ready to take to the utility area.

Large garbage or trash receptacles can hold ski gear in the summer and summer clothes in the winter.

A large, attractive wicker basket (with a lid) can be lined with a covered plastic trash can or plastic bag and used to hold a few extra pounds of sugar, flour, beans, rice or anything, for that matter. These baskets can also hold dish towels, cleaning cloths or diapers. Baskets can be placed decoratively on the floor in any room.

So if space is a problem, look between, under and behind. The added feature here is that you get more storage space per square foot of floor space. Take another look at that floor—it's a great storage alternative.

DROP IT INTO A DRAWER

The storage uses for drawers are somewhat more obvious than those for hanging or floors, but if you think creatively you can come up with some novel uses. Anything from paper towels to spices can be stored effectively in a drawer. Jewelry can be kept tangle free in a drawer by storing it in ice cube trays.

A drawer can give you extra counter space or provide additional table space. Here's how: Open a drawer and place a cookie sheet or cutting board on top. Close the drawer as far as it will go and there's additional work space for you.

For inexpensive drawers, stack two covered orange or apple boxes. (Ask your grocer to save some of these boxes for you. While certain stores recycle them, others toss them out. Some merchants will sell them for a nominal fee. Call a few grocery

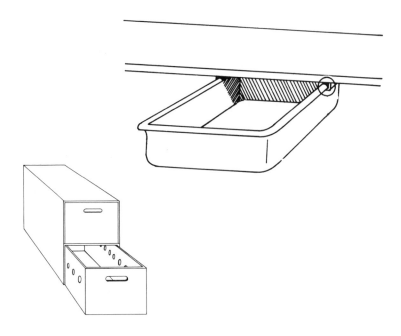

Drawers can be made with dishpans and U-shaped molding

stores and see what their policy is.) Cut out one end panel on each of the two lids, and put the lids on the boxes. Stack one box on top of the other, and cover the sides, top and back with self-adhesive paper. Attach a drawer pull to the front of each drawer, and you've got instant and inexpensive drawers. Drawers can also be constructed under existing shelves using U-shaped molding and dishpans.

At discount stores there's a plethora of inexpensive drawer units. Cardboard shoe files hold nine shoe boxes that function like drawers. Especially useful are the four-drawer cardboard chests and plastic drawers that come in many mix, match and stack sizes.

Virtually anything, providing it's not too large, can go into a drawer. Of all the storage options, though, drawers are the hardest to maintain. Often they become open pits in which to dump anything. A quick shove, the drawer is closed, and the unsightly mess is out of view. Drawers almost seem to invite clutter.

DIVIDE AND CONQUER

The answer to functional drawer space is to use plenty of drawer dividers. Inexpensive plastic ones in a range of sizes are widely available at variety stores. Cardboard boxes can also be cut to fit the drawers, thus giving everything a specific place.

Actually, anything that is hollow and rectangular (or square) is a potential divider. Dishpans, ice cube bins, plastic liners for windowbox planters, cutlery trays, four-sided napkin holders and cosmetic trays are a few alternatives to regular drawer dividers. Cardboard boxes are free if you're pressed for cash. Throughout the course of this book, you will learn specific ways to use drawer dividers.

I had one particular dresser drawer that was always a mess. It seemed that every week I had to completely redo the whole thing. I was using a few drawer dividers, so I couldn't understand my predicament. After analyzing the situation, I discovered that one drawer divider held three different types of things. Shortly after I separated them, they were once again piled in a heap.

I removed everything from the drawer and grouped like items together. Next, using small cardboard boxes and plastic shoe boxes, I made individual compartments for each category. Because I was able to cut the cardboard to just the right size, every inch of drawer space was used. The drawer is now extremely functional and stays organized.

There are a few helpful rules to follow when using drawer dividers. Fill up drawers with dividers as you would place pieces of a puzzle, using any container that's square or rectangluar in shape. Drawer dividers should be almost as tall as the drawer they're put in. Otherwise, you'll have a level mass of confusion and the drawer dividers will be adding to it.

When you're organizing tall things in drawer dividers (dishwashing liquid, spray paint, a vertical cluster of screwdrivers, bottles of corn syrup, molasses, soy sauce, etc.) the divider should be 4 or 5 inches tall. That will keep the contents of the divider from tipping over.

How to keep the drawer divider from sliding around? Bar mat is a rubber mesh that restaurants use as shelf liner. You can buy it by the foot at a restaurant supply house. You can also purchase a similar product at places that sell supplies for recreational vehicles. (It is used in RVs to keep things from sliding and shifting while the vehicle is in motion.) Bar mat comes in all different colors. You can throw it in the washing machine or the dishwasher. It's a one-time investment.

Bar mat is good for storing anything glass because it cushions the shelf and allows for air ventilation. It's also sturdy enough for pan storage. Put a piece in the crisper of the refrigerator. It keeps moisture from forming on the fruits and vegetables. Also, it's perfectly suited for storing canned goods on painted shelves. The bar mat keeps the shelf from staining, chipping or rusting.

A small piece of bar mat placed under bookends or the baby in the high chair will keep them from slipping. (When the baby is learning to feed himself it helps to put a small piece of bar mat under his dish and booster chair, too.)

As far as drawers are concerned, divide and conquer is the rule!

SHELVE IT

There have been whole books written on the subject of shelving, so you can see the popularity and adaptability of this storage option. There are a few guidelines, though, that can help you make the most efficient use of your shelves.

Shelves, like drawers, can be divided and categorized giving everything a well-defined, well-confined place. Small items can be categorized and placed in bins, dishpans, buckets, boxes, etc. These organizers can also be used as slide-out trays to make things on a shelf easy to reach.

Shelves that are too deep result in hard-to-use areas, because things need to be stored one in front of the other. Standard 12-inch shelves will give you one-motion storage and provide a fast, functional system. Narrow shelves are especially important for high storage because these areas are harder to see and to reach. Wider shelves are okay for low storage as long as you keep high priority things in front to provide one-motion storage. If you're already stuck with deep, awkward shelves, sometimes it helps to put the stored items into sturdy boxes that you can slide out. This way everything is easier to see and reach.

Stacked items should be placed on lower shelves, so they don't topple over when you remove them. A good rule is never to stack more than two high, three maximum. Large things that are not

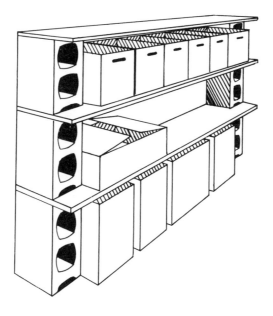

Shelving units can be made from particle board and cement blocks

too heavy and that you can remove with one motion are good candidates for storage on high shelves.

Ideally, shelving should be adjustable to accommodate objects that are varied in size. Adjustable shelves can be mounted on a wall or other vertical surface with track and bracket fittings. You can also suspend shelves with rope or chain from a ceiling.

Shelves need not be expensive. Snap together shelves (metal and industrial strength plastic), recycled bookcases, heavy cardboard shelves and particle board shelves (stacked on bricks, cement blocks or large food cans) are a few of the less expensive alternatives. A small, freestanding shelf put inside a closet can be especially beneficial in children's rooms.

Open shelves can add to the cluttered appearance of a home. Unless you are a naturally neat person, keep your shelves covered with a door, a blind or a folding screen.

So there you have four storage options. As you read the many storage ideas in this book, keep these four alternatives in mind.

They will help you adapt any of the following ideas to the architecture and physical layout of your home, dorm or apartment. Even if you have an efficiency apartment, the four storage options will open up untold areas of unused space.

CHAPTER TWENTY

Storing the Tools of Your Trade

P eople who love hobbies can easily have a mess on their hands, and on their floors and tables as well. I know many folks who avoid creative projects simply because of the general disorder and storage problems that result. What a shame to miss out on the fun of creating for fear of a little chaos and inconvenience. A little mayhem never hurt anybody, but using the basic organizing principles we can eliminate a lot of unnecessary clutter.

SEWING AND CRAFTS

Not only can sewing and crafts litter up a house, there are seemingly hundreds of things to store. Have you ever rummaged through a box of fabric trying to find the right piece? And what do you do with miniature novelties or the tips to stylus writing pens? What about seam bindings, hem facings, bias tape, elastic, buttons, trims, ribbons, lace, felt, glue, thread, bobbins, scissors — a person could drown in the debris. It can get complicated. However, order and organization will simplify things. Remember, our main premise is to give everything a well-defined place.

Storing Fabric

Let's start with sewing. The main storage problem I've had with sewing has always been storing fabric and patterns. If you have a *lot* of fabric to be stored, here's an idea you might like.

Purchase a covered cardboard storage box (the kind you put together yourself) or get a cardboard produce box. You're going to make miniature "bolts" to wrap your fabric around, and store them inside this box. Measure the long side of the box and the height of the box. Cut several pieces of corrugated cardboard

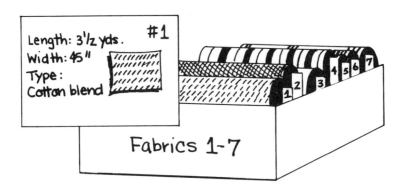

Handy fabric storage with swatch card

just 1 to 2 inches shorter than the measured length and 2 inches shorter than the height of the box. (Your bolts will be less likely to bend if the corrugation runs vertically rather than horizontally.)

Once that is done, measure and record the widths and lengths of your fabric pieces. When you have made as many bolts as you need, wrap each measured length of fabric around a separate bolt, and secure the ends with two straight pins or staples. Now you can flip through your fabric just as you would file folders.

To make this method even more efficient, here are a couple of things you can do: Cut a small swatch from each piece of fabric. Secure the swatch with glue or staples to a 3″ × 5″ card. Then, on the index card, write the length and width of the fabric and the type of material. Number the index cards, and number the fabric bolts to correspond. The cards can be kept in a file box or in a magnetic photo album. Both methods allow for deletions as the fabric is used and additions when new fabric is purchased. The index cards can be categorized by type of fabric.

Instead of the numbering method, you may want to sort your fabric by type or fabric content (e.g., polyester-cotton blends in one box, wool in another). Just be sure to write on the index card in which box the particular fabric can be found.

You will also need one box to hold large, irregularly shaped scraps that cannot be wrapped around a bolt. Cut swatches from these pieces, and make up index cards as previously described.

Having all your fabric samples together in a book or file makes it handy to take them to a fabric store when you want to choose new fabric to match what you already have at home. The samples are also handy to have when choosing new sewing patterns, and you always know exactly what you have on hand.

I recommend going into this much detail *only* if you have a lot of fabric and if you use it often. If you need a piece of fabric once every few months or so, a little rummaging is okay. Don't spend time to organize something unless you're going to get your time investment back by saving time in the long run.

There are less elaborate ways to store fabric. Rolled pieces of yardage can be stored in a cardboard shoe file. The shoe file sits on a shelf or the floor and will hold many yards of fabric and keep it all visible.

The hanging storage alternative can also be used for fabric. Individual pieces of stored material can be folded and hung on clamping pants hangers. Many fabric stores use this method. If you've got plenty of hanging room, this alternative would work very well.

Another hanging device, a purse file, hangs on a closet rod and has eight large, clear pockets in which to store purses. This purse file will hold many rolled-up pieces of fabric and keep them all visible. This will use up approximately 10 inches of closet space.

Of course, fabric can also be rolled up and stored in boxes. Staple a small piece of paper to one of the corners of the fabric indicating how big the piece is, fabric content, or whatever information is necessary. If you have several pieces of fabric, you can categorize them by color or fabric content.

Storing Patterns

You probably don't know this, but pattern envelopes are made by the same company that makes game boxes and puzzle boxes. And patterns can be stored efficiently, too. Everyone who sews knows that patterns only fit in the pattern envelope before they are used. Once you've used a pattern, refolding it to fit back into the envelope takes more skill that the actual sewing.

Before I give you some storage ideas, though, I want to pass along something a woman once asked me when I was telling a class how to store patterns. She said, "Why would you want to save patterns in the first place?"

Good question. How many dresses or outfits will you really wear if they're made out of the same pattern? Now, if you're an expert sewer you're probably intermingling patterns and perhaps even sewing for other people. If you have several children and do a lot of sewing, you'll certainly want to keep all the children's size patterns. My point is simply this—think before you act. Don't just automatically organize something because you have it. Do you really need it? Are you going to use it? If you can answer, "Yes," then you're ready to hear some organizing ideas. Here are three ways patterns can be stored. The first is especially effective if you have a *lot* of patterns.

Take the pattern pieces and put them into a 9″ × 6″ manila envelope. On the envelope write the pattern brand name and number (Simplicity 6184). Punch and reinforce holes on the left-hand side of the envelope and place it in a 9″ × 12″ loose-leaf ring binder. Take the original pattern envelope and put it into a 6″ × 9″ loose-leaf ring binder. (Punch and reinforce holes on the left-hand side of the pattern envelope.) If you prefer, you can open the envelope so the pictures and specifications are visible at one glance.

As you place the original pattern envelopes in the binder, you will probably want to arrange them the way they are arranged in the pattern catalogs—according to gender and size. Do not sort the patterns by brand or number. The manila envelopes, however, are filed by brand, numerically.

When you're all finished, you have your own homemade pattern catalog. Leaf through it until you find the pattern you want. Then, referring to the brand and pattern number on the envelope, go to your filed manila envelopes and pull out the one you want. The pattern catalog is handy to take to a fabric store when you want to buy fabric for one of your patterns.

A second system also works well, and is my favorite. I have a lot of patterns, but not hundreds. Take each pattern envelope and cut it open so that all the pattern specifications are visible. Glue this onto a 9″ × 12″ manila envelope, and put the pattern pieces inside. Again, arrange the patterns according to size and type. You now have a more durable way to store your patterns, and the pattern pieces are easier to replace. Patterns stored in this way will fit in a file drawer, a cardboard file box, or a standard magazine file, which will hold several.

The third idea for pattern storing is to open up the pattern envelope and mount it on the front of a file folder. Put the pattern pieces inside and file it as you would file a folder. To keep all the pattern pieces inside the folder you can sew up the sides, or glue or tape them. You can purchase file folders that are sealed on the sides, but they're more expensive.

Some sewing experts tell me that after they make an outfit they put some fabric scraps and a few extra buttons from the completed project right into the pattern envelope. Then when a repair is needed, they can find what they need.

Notions, Novelties and Craft Supplies

My life is over if Ziploc storage bags are ever phased out of production. Here's another way I depend on them. I use a lot of felt, and I got tired of hunting through a box full of felt scraps every time I needed a certain color. So, I bought a box of the gallon-size Ziploc food storage bags. I reinforced the left-hand edge of the bag with mailing tape and punched three holes down the side—like notebook paper. I sorted the felt by color and placed each color in a separate bag. Then I put three loose binder rings through the holes. I now have a nice, neat book of felt. The durability of those bags is amazing. I have used my felt book for several years and I have not had to replace one bag.

One woman liked this idea so well, she made a Ziploc book to hold Barbie doll oufits—one outfit per page. She says it's the greatest thing ever! Another family used a Ziploc book to store paper dolls.

This same idea can help you store things such as elastic, seam bindings, ribbons, trims, laces and embroidery floss using the quart-size Ziploc storage bags. But don't stop there. These books can also hold latch hook and crewel yarns, pom-poms, wiggly eyes, costume jewelry, scarves, even different grades of sandpaper. The books will fit into a dishpan that sits on a shelf. They will also nestle nicely in a drawer, or you can even hang a book up using one of the rings.

I use plastic shoe boxes for things such as bias tape, bindings, zippers, buttons and trims. The boxes stack nicely and, even though they are labeled as to content, I can see at a glance what is in them.

Most of my zippers are recycled, taken from discarded clothing. I measure each zipper, mark the length on masking tape, and put the tape on the bottom edge of the zipper. Each zipper is folded and secured with a rubber band.

The trims, lace, ribbon and bindings are wrapped around "mini bolts" I have cut from lightweight cardboard. This way I can flip through the standing bolts and choose what I want.

Another see-through shoe box contains my collection of buttons. The buttons are sorted by color and put into quart-size Ziploc bags—red buttons in one bag, brown in another, etc. Button sets or identical buttons are fastened together with hairpins (they're easy to bend). This way I don't have to spend time looking for a set. A plastic shoe box will hold hundreds of buttons.

A cardboard shoe file will hold nine plastic shoe boxes and give you handy drawers for all these notions. If you have a chest of drawers, the plastic shoe boxes are sturdy drawer dividers.

Skeins of yarn can be stored very decoratively. Open baskets full of yarn add a warm, charming look to a room. Or hang up a wooden wine rack and store colorful skeins of yarn in each compartment.

Large, round cardboard ice cream cartons (from Baskin-Robbins or your local ice cream parlor) can be stacked on their sides on a shelf and used as bins for extra skeins. (Did I say round?)

If you're storing large amounts of yarn you might need to put it in covered boxes and store according to color. A cardboard shoe file will comfortably hold approximately eighteen skeins of yarn and make it easy to see and reach.

Straight knitting needles can be stored in a long aluminum foil box. You can also weave long knitting needles through a loosely woven placemat. The mat holds about ten or twelve pairs of needles. You can roll up the mat for storage, or hang it up.

Browse through a fabric, yarn or craft shop. There are many products available that can help bring order out of anyone's sewing basket—zippered pouches that hold crochet hooks and circular knitting needles, bobbins for embroidery floss, yarn pallets for crewel embroidery and needlepoint projects. And those metal parts cabinets are an organizer's dream. They come in all sizes, with all different sized drawers. This is a great place for all those little "what do I do with this?" things. Just make sure the drawers are well labeled.

Sewing boxes or cash, tool or tackle boxes also make great

carryalls for sewing or craft projects. You will be able to find a size to fit any need. These same containers are excellent totes for all kinds of office supplies.

I hate the get-ready and clean-up of craft and sewing projects. I'd much rather leave everything out until the job is completed. However, with lots of little fingers around I can't leave things unattended. So whenever I can, I use a box or dishpan to hold all my supplies. To get ready, I grab the box. To clean up, I dump everything back in and put it out of sight. Also, I write myself a short note as to what I'm working on when I set the project aside. Next time I'm ready to work I don't have to waste time wondering where I was.

Here are a few time saving hints I use for crafting:

- Round toothpicks are used as straight pins to keep knitted or crocheted seams together for sewing.
- Photocopy directions or graph charts. That way you can mark them up and note stopping points.
- Rubber-tipped bobby pins make great stitch markers.
- Cut patterns to be traced from old plastic lids. The plastic won't bind, fray or tear and will last forever.

My hobby is sewing, and most of these tips have been specifically about patterns, fabric and notions. However, the same principles can be applied by painters (with proper precautions regarding combustibles), woodworkers, musicians, writers and collectors. Refer to The Four Storage Options chapter to organize your hobby.

THE WORKROOM

If you're rebuilding a Model A or sharpening lawn mower blades, you probably haven't found this chapter too helpful so far. There are ways, though, to keep a garage or workroom from looking like one. (My organized next-door neighbor has a two-car garage that is so neat you could easily make a U-turn in it.)

Lawn tools can be hung up on a peg board or between two closely placed nails. There are also hanging gadgets you can purchase. Check your local hardware and discount stores.

Floor storage is also possible. Put the rakes, hoes, shovels, etc. into a galvanized garbage can, and secure the can's handle to a wall to keep it from tipping over. This will give large tools a well-confined, well-defined place without using much space.

Dishpans can work wonders in a workroom. Have one for plumbing needs, one for electrical, one for socket wrenches, and one for painting and wallpapering accessories. Label the dishpans, and keep them on a shelf. Slide out the container, and choose what you need. When something needs to be put away, it's just as easy to toss it into a dishpan as it is to put it on the workbench "for now."

Organize garden tools in a metal garbage can when hanging space is limited

Metal parts cabinets with plastic drawers and a variety of other organizers are widely available to hold all your nuts and bolts. Jar lids can be nailed to the underside of a shelf and jars full of nails, screws and washers can be screwed right into the lids.

Have a special jar or container for screws that you find on the kitchen floor (or wherever). They must have fallen out of something! When you do discover a missing screw, you'll know where to look for it. And if you have a specific container, a houseful of miscellaneous screws won't be scattered here and there or thrown into junk drawers.

Screw top jars with lids fastened to the underside of a shelf give see-through storage for small items

Whether the tools of your trade are knitting needles or power saws, you can bring order out of confusion by using the basic organizing principles!

PART FIVE

CONCLUSION

CHAPTER TWENTY-ONE

Where Do I Start?

I f my head were flat, I'd probably store things on it," lamented Mrs. X. "I really don't care for housework. I'd much rather read a book than scrub the floor, but things are drastically out of control! I have to do something. Where do I start?"

Every day I get calls and letters from people all over the country, usually with the same request, "Where do I start?" To the inquirer I say, "What one area is really bothering you?" The standard answer is, "Everything!"

If you feel, as these people do, that the walls of Jericho are tumbling down around you, take heart. You can get control over your surroundings, but you have to want success enough to exercise patience, persistence and energy. As one caterpillar said to the other caterpillar, "You have to want to fly so much that you're willing to give up being a caterpillar!" If you're ready to become a butterfly, you'll be able to do it.

DECIDE WHERE TO START

Deciding where to start is always the hardest part, especially when so many things (and people) are screaming for your attention. To find your best place to start, begin with this checklist:

- I am able to keep the house picked up.
- I am able to keep the laundry current.
- Meals are well prepared and served regularly.
- The kitchen is usually in good order.
- Bathrooms are cleaned and straightened regularly.
- I am able to keep entry areas clean and tidy.

Before you begin any organizational project, make sure that

these six areas are under control. They are the bare essentials that will keep your home running smoothly. They are the most important, so try not to neglect or overlook them.

If several of these are a problem, the first three (pickup, laundry and meals) are paramount. Begin with only one of them. Make your choice, and determine that you will concentrate your efforts on that one area. Force yourself, if necessary, to keep that one chosen area current for six weeks. Try not to let any other areas bother you. For now, you will work on one thing at a time.

The principle of concentrating attention on one chosen area worked very well for one home manager. I'll let her tell her own story:

"For years I was frustrated and discouraged. My house was disorganized. I had grandchildren I wanted to sew for. My living room needed redecorating. I wanted to assemble a photograph album for my mother. My part-time job took extra hours from my day. There were so many things I wanted to do. Other people did them — I just talked about doing them. These overwhelming feelings gradually led to depression.

"I would browse through fabric shops looking for upholstery material one day, clean out a kitchen cupboard the next day, cut out a pattern for my granddaughter, and on and on, never finishing anything. Then I tried to concentrate and to focus on the living room.

"Sometimes it was hard, but I forced myself to concentrate on the job at hand. Step by step I am getting control of my life and loving it."

At the end of six weeks, check your progress. If you think you can maintain this area, choose another and go on. However, if you're still struggling, give it another six weeks. Don't be discouraged. You are probably trying to undo bad habits that took years to develop.

Think about the oyster. At first a grain of sand under its shell is a bothersome irritation. In time, however, this annoying kernel becomes a precious pearl.

If the top six areas are not causing problems, and you still feel defeated, further probing is necessary. Take a minute to sit down and collect your thoughts. Make a written list of everything that's bothering you. (If you're feeling especially brave, ask your family what they would like to see changed. If they feel a part of the plan, they may be more cooperative.)

Take a look at your checklist and put a check by the things that are:

- Causing a lot of interruptions. (These items are wasting your time and causing you to spend more hours on housework than you need to.)
- A source of great irritation for your spouse or other family members. (These things are giving rise to tension and anxiety.)
- Really bothering you. (These items are giving you "that feeling." They are making you uncomfortable.)

These checked entries should be given top priority. If many things are checked, pick one at random and begin.

Once you can see (via your written list) what's bothering you, you can get a handle on it and begin your six-week program, if necessary.

If, after using the checklist, you still can't decide where to begin, just go about your normal routine for a few days. Be mindful, though, of the trouble spots that continually create a snag in your daily living. Surely you will discover something so irritating that you have to do something about it.

For example, after our children started coming, I began to really feel bogged down by the washing. At three or four in the afternoon I could feel this black cloud hovering over me. I still had wet clothes waiting to be dried and dirty clothes needing to be washed. My outlook was dim because I didn't want an evening of finishing, folding, and putting away the wash.

I hated the wash and I hated those feelings. I knew the wash wasn't going to go away, so I had to change my approach or be miserable for the rest of my washing career.

I decided to wash on Monday, Wednesday, Friday and Saturday (optionally). That way, I would have three or four days when I didn't have to worry or feel guilty about it. Planning the days didn't help a lot, though. I was finding that after I fed the children and bathed the baby, I wasn't even able to *start* the washing until 9 or 10 A.M. There was enough time during the busy early morning hours to throw a load into the washer, but there wasn't enough time to sort, pretreat stains, check pockets and turn ev-

---

BEING ORGANIZED IS GOOD FOR YOUR HEALTH

1. Children, as well as adults, feel more secure in an organized, orderly environment.

2. Frustrations (trying to find something that's not where it should be), irritations (running out of a key ingredient while preparing dinner), and worry (knowing you were going to do something, but unsure what exactly it was), drain energy.

3. Think back to the last time you had control of your home. Didn't you have a certain peace of mind? That's mental good health.

---

erything right side out. So I started sorting and pretreating the wash the night before.

With this system I could have all the clothes washed and put away by 10 A.M. Winning the washday battle was such a triumph! I felt like I had really conquered something.

One day I went to pick up two girls who were going to spend a week at our home. Their mother was concerned that they wouldn't have enough clothing with them. She said, "You wash all the time, don't you?" I smiled to myself knowing I was freed from having to wash all the time. I no longer had that feeling of despair in the bottom of my stomach. I felt so successful it spilled over into other areas of my housework.

DECIDE WHEN TO START

After you've decided where you're going to start, make a firm resolve when to start. Think of getting organized as a hobby and work on that basis. Set a firm appointment with yourself. Treat this appointment with respect. Unless an emergency comes up, do not cancel it.

You'll be surprised how much can be accomplished if you only work fifteen minutes a day or thirty minutes a day three times a week. Do not over-program! Once you get going, you might be tempted to go on for hours, but don't do it. Move steadily and slowly and maintain each space as you move onto your next area.

If you do not have a large block of time available, keep your working area isolated. For example, do one drawer in the kitchen or one shelf. Don't tear your whole kitchen apart and dig in. A large mess is overwhelming and can easily discourage you. Take things little by little, and chip away at your chores.

I once read an ad for an oil company that said, "When you've done one thing, you've done something." Always remember the fifteen- or thirty-minute appointment you kept, and savor your successes. Forget what is unfinished, and be proud of the one thing you did.

As they say in butterfly school, "The harder you try, the higher you fly!"

CHAPTER TWENTY-TWO

The Beginning

Once upon a time there was a woman who went shopping for a new blanket. The shopkeeper showed her the very finest blanket in his shop. "Oh, it's beautiful. It's just what I wanted," said the woman. But her excitement turned to disappointment when she saw that the blanket measured 8' × 8'. "I'm afraid it's just too big for my double bed," she wailed.

"On the contrary," said the shopkeeper. "You need a blanket this large. You see, it's the extra yardage — the part of the blanket that hangs over the edge — that really keeps you warm."

And so it is with our homes. That extra margin of order and organization gives us the "warmth" of security and peace of mind.

In my role as a home manager, my main goal is to provide my family with a tidy, comfortable home. I want to make home a place where we all want to be. Confusion and disorder drive people away. Everyone wants to be surrounded by a peaceful atmosphere.

The only way to achieve this is through organization! Yes, there are times when things are a mess, but when the underlying things are in order, surface messes are easy to clean up. When everything has a well-defined place, it doesn't take long to put things back where they belong. So, you see the chaos never lasts long, and I quickly return my family and myself to peaceful surroundings. When things are organized you can act on occasional crises when they arise. But without planning, everything becomes a crisis.

Children, as well as adults, feel more secure in a home that is consistent and orderly. They know what to expect and what is expected. How can we teach our children responsibility if we fail to be responsible at home?

When your mind is at peace, the time you spend doing anything is high-quality time. Think back to a time when you had control of your home, when things were in order. Didn't you have a certain peace of mind? Isn't that wonderful feeling worth having at least most of the time? You can do it!

Now that you've come this far you know how order can be achieved. You have your family interested, and you want to do it. But there's one last stumbling block. How do you get the energy to carry it off?

The most common complaint I hear from people is that they have no energy. They're tired. They can't get up at 4 A.M. and work until midnight like so-and-so can. A truly organized person shouldn't have to.

There are, of course, many reasons for tiredness. I have read several studies about fatigue and have learned some interesting facts.

- Tiredness is emotionally induced 90 percent of the time.
- Frustrations, irritations and worry drain energy.
- The mere contemplation of work causes more fatigue than the job itself.
- Fatigue is not always related to the amount of energy we use but to how much we dislike the task. Procrastination, by the way, adds dislike to our chores. The longer we put off an important project, the more threatening and unattractive it becomes.
- The people who are most tired are those whose behavior and work methods demonstrate disorder.
- Proper diet and regular exercise are necessary to fight fatigue.

The organizing system you have just learned is the solution. This system will help you reach your goals, and reaching your goals is what brings happiness. And happiness is the best stimulant!

THE WISEST INVESTMENT

Imagine just for a minute that you have a very good friend who comes to your home every day. Every time this friend comes, he gives you $86,400. He asks no questions of you. He only requires that you spend or invest the whole amount, because what you don't spend has to be returned to him. Wouldn't you spend every cent, knowing he would be back the next day with the same amount?

Well, each of us has such a friend. His name is Time. Every morning he deposits 86,400 seconds in our account. What is not spent is forever lost, never to return. It is up to us to use these precious seconds wisely. We must invest them in our lives. When we waste time we are wasting ourselves.

Stop wasting the happiness and security that can be yours. Put into action a program that makes getting organized exciting and attractive. Getting things in order not only puts more time in your life, it will put more life in your time.

Like you, I have days when I feel overwhelmed and shell-shocked. It's on those days I remember the words of author and motivational speaker Zig Ziglar: "A big shot is simply a little shot who kept shooting."

INDEX

More Great Books to Help You Get The Most Out Of Life!

Deniece Schofield's Kitchen Organization Tips and Secrets—Make work in your kitchen more organized and productive—from storage to cleaning to grocery shopping and more! You'll discover time-saving strategies to integrate kitchen work into your hectic schedule and suggestions for making the most of the space you have.
#70326/$12.99/240 pages/50 b&w illus./paperback

Stephanie Culp's 12-Month Organizer and Project Planner—This is the get-it-done planner! If you have projects you're burning to start or yearning to finish, you'll zoom toward accomplishment by using these forms, "To-Do" lists, checklists and calendars.
#70274/$12.99/192 pages/paperback

Is There Life After Housework?—All you need to take the dread out of housework are some ingenious ideas and a little inspiration. You'll find both in Aslett's revolutionary approach designed to free you from the drudgery of housework!
#10292/$11.99/216 pages/250 b&w illus./paperback

How to Get Organized When You Don't Have the Time—You keep meaning to organize the closet and clean out the garage, but who has the time? Culp combines proven time-management principles with practical ideas to help you clean up key trouble spots in a hurry.
01354/$14.99/216 pages/illus./paperback

Streamlining Your Life—Tired of the fast-track life? Stephanie Culp comes to the rescue with quick, practical, good-humored and helpful solutions to life's biggest problem—not having enough time. You'll get practical solutions to recurring problems, plus a 5-point plan to help you take care of tedious tasks. *#10238/$11.99/142 pages/paperback*

Make Your House Do the Housework, Revised Edition—Take advantage of new work-saving products, materials and approaches to make your house keep itself in order. You'll discover page after page of practical, environmentally-friendly new ideas and methods for minimizing home cleaning and maintenance. This book includes charts that rate materials and equipment. Plus, you'll find suggestions for approaching everything from simple do-it-yourself projects to remodeling jobs of all sizes.
#70293/$14.99/208 pages/215 b&w illus./paperback

You can Find More Time for Yourself Every Day—Professionals, working mothers, college students—if you're in a hurry, you need this time-saving guide! Quizzes, tests and charts will show you how to make the most of your minutes!
#70258/$12.99/208 pages/paperback

Don Aslett's Clutter-Free! Finally and Forever—Free yourself of unnecessary stuff that chokes your home and clogs your life! If you feel owned by your belongings, this book is for you. Discover incredible excuses people use for allowing clutter, how to beat the "no-time" excuse, how to determine what's junk, how to prevent recluttering and much more!
#70306/$12.99/224 pages/50 illus./paperback